S0-AYX-284

Live Your Life from the Front Seat

*Accomplish Magnificent Things
in your life, relationships and career*

Jessica Butts, MA

Copyright © 2015 Jessica Butts

Live Your Life from the Front Seat

Accomplish Magnificent Things in your life, relationships and career

All rights reserved. No part of this book may be reproduced, stored
in a retrieval system or transmitted by any other means without the
written permission of the publisher and author.

Jessica Butts

www.jessicabutts.com

ISBN: 0989704955

ISBN: 978-0-9897049-5-3

Library of Congress: 2015940153

Cover design by Milena Creative

Interior text design and printing by Gorham Printing

Legacy ONE AUTHORS

Kirkland, WA

www.legacyoneauthors.com

. . . .

Dedication

. . . .

This book is dedicated to all the
women and men who have stories
similar to mine and
have not yet taken the steps to live a
life you love...you can do it.

We only get one life on earth.

Please, please make it the best you
possibly can
so you do not regret one minute of it.

Acknowledgments

I want to thank Brian, my ex-husband, for a 20-year relationship that has influenced who I am today. Our relationship has made it possible for me to do the work I do and to help people not make the same mistakes we did in our marriage.

To my book coach and good friend, Karen: your love and presence in my life has allowed me to dream big and take action. This has been quite a journey, my friend, and one I could not have done without you.

To my mom, Barbara, for showing me what it looks like to be a strong woman with an uncompromising work ethic. Your presence has taught me how to be a tough, yet humble, woman of God.

To my Pop, Clare, for showing me (not just telling me) that I could do anything I wanted. Anything! I am not sure I would be here in my life without your soft, loving and supportive presence in my life. You are truly an amazing man; thank you for being my Pop.

I must always and until the end of time thank my sister, Erica. There has always been one loving constant in my life and that has been you. Thank you for the shoulder to cry on, more laughs than there are stars in the sky and being my life-long partner in love, friendship and sisterhood.

Contents

Letter to my readers

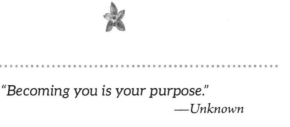

"Becoming you is your purpose."
—*Unknown*

I am you! Just so you know right up front, **I am weird** and my hunch is you are, too.

I have been misunderstood for most of my life by everyone I hold dear: my mother, most of my friends, my ex-husband and my professional colleagues. I've always thought there was something wrong with me until I realized the exact opposite. The truth is, I have a personality Type that is shared by only 25% of the population. I'm Intuitive.

Have you had a similar experience throughout your life? I bet most of you reading this book have had a life experience similar to mine. You, too, are probably an Intuitive person. I know this because you likely found this book in the self-help section of a bookstore, which is where a lot of Intuitive people hang out. Or, your good friend—also an Intuitive Type—recommended you read this book. Given that we belong to an exclusive segment of the people walking this planet, we stick together. Throughout this book I am going to teach you much, *much* more about your awesomeness (as every Type is awesome in its own way), so keep reading. The information in the pages between the front and back covers of this book will change your life. Guaranteed!

Everything in this book is the culmination of the most meaningful relationships and experiences of my life. This includes growing up in a middle class family, attending college, getting married when I had no idea who I was, working in corporate human resources for 15 years, attending graduate school and becoming a psychotherapist, starting a private therapy practice and making some difficult decisions to change my life at age 40 so I could experience the life I was meant to live.

My desire is for you to do the same—live the life God/Universe intended for you. Right up front, I want you to know that I believe in God, but I also believe in universal energy so I will use them interchangeably throughout the book. Some of you may have a different name for the source of your spiritual guidance and connection. Some names I've heard are higher power, the Universe or source. Please know that the exact name or the words used are secondary. What truly matters is that you foster the connection and the relationship outside yourself that gives you peace and wisdom to become who you really are!

In order to flourish, we each have unique brilliance that we have to figure out, explore and accept. This book will push you, challenge you and possibly even scare you at times. It's an invitation to discover the truth about yourself, your unique brilliance and how you are meant to be living your life.

Most people don't know who they are until they are close to 40 years old. They're fulfilling the demands and obligations of their lives, and for the most part, everything seems to be going along well. They have no reason to question how they're living their lives, until something happens that gets their attention. Then they start to wonder if, in fact, they are expressing their unique brilliance and best self. On my 40th birthday I woke up on Maui knowing for sure that I would be ending my 20-year marriage. That decision was the result of a five-year journey of following the process I share in this book to create and live my most authentic life. It's been a challenging, yet magnificent, journey.

Many of my clients have said something like, "I wish I had an owner's manual for my life." Well, here it is! This book contains all the best tools I have used with myself and my clients to help us get clear about who we are.

We are all reinventing ourselves: evolving, growing, and changing every day. But at our core, we are who we are and there is much about us that will not change. A giraffe can want to live in a pond and sit on a lily pad all day. Or, a frog can want to eat leaves from a tall tree. But both animals are who they are and it's impossible for them to be anything else.

. . . .

"Be unapologetically
who you are!"
—*Jessica Butts*

. . . .

The same is true for me and for you. We have Innate gifts and abilities and we have learned behaviors that shape who we are. Once we can start to embrace our innateness we can start to build a magnificent life for ourselves.

The work I'm inviting you to do in this book—fully and truly embracing who you are—can be hard, but believe me, it is also incredibly liberating. Discovering that you are hardwired, to be certain ways can be challenging and hard to hear, especially if your Innate makeup is to be sharp or crass with strangers, or unorganized, quick tempered, cautious and reluctant to change. But truly embracing who you are—the good and the not so great—is powerful. Life gets a lot easier and more fulfilling when frogs finally embrace that they'll never leave the pond and their diet will always be bugs. When they stop straining their necks and wishing they could eat leaves in tall trees, they discover the magic and awesomeness of being a frog.

It has taken me 41 years to get to where I am today. I decided to write this book because sharing my journey, knowledge and the tools I've acquired along the way can and will change lives. I want to help you explore who you are, get honest, get real and hopefully inspire you enough to make some changes in your life. If you have ever wished you were someone else, my hope is that you will never do that again, and instead, embrace who you are.

Are you ready to go on this journey with me to discover yourself?

Let's begin.

Introduction

"Sometimes the people around you won't understand your journey. They don't need to, it's not for them."
—*Unknown*

Have you ever had the thought, "Is it possible that I'm destined for something greater than what I'm doing right now?"

Have you ever been told that you should be doing anything other than what you're doing now? You might hear statements like, "You're not smart enough, fast enough, strong enough." No matter the words, they all lead to the same belief of, "I'm not enough." Period.

Have you ever felt inadequate, dissatisfied or unfulfilled with your life?

I have. I know these feelings intimately.

Something I know with absolute certainty is that you are destined to Accomplish Magnificent Things in your life.

If you had known me in 2006, you would have thought that I had it all together. I was working in corporate human resources making good money. I had a nice house, a nice car and to all outward appearances, my marriage was rock solid. Everything looked great.

Except that it wasn't.

Although I had a high paying job with all the perks, I felt unbelievably unfulfilled and unhappy. I tried to tell myself that all was well and that I should be happy doing what I was doing and in my relationship. For quite a while I believed what I kept telling myself.

I grew up believing I wasn't an interesting person—that who I was and what I was doing in the world were unimportant. In my most intimate relationships, especially my marriage, I was frightened to rock the boat. I was terrified of how people would judge me. I was afraid that the life I had created couldn't handle the truth of who I really am. I was right. I created a life that didn't allow me to shine. I had to dull myself in order to fit in.

One day my husband, the only man I had ever had a real relationship with, came home and told me he wasn't sure he loved me and that he wanted to move out. I was devastated and shocked. I spent the next few months of my life feeling powerless, confused, frantic and lost. I spent countless hours sitting on my kitchen floor sobbing, not knowing what to do and wondering, "How did I get to this place in my life?"

But, somewhere deep inside my heart I knew that I was supposed to be Accomplishing Magnificent Things. God designed me to live magnificently; shouldn't I be doing that? There on my kitchen floor, I started to pay attention and dare to believe in the magnificence that awaited me, if only I'd embrace the necessary changes.

I am now thankful for those moments of personal torture because they became the catalyst for me to wake myself up from the fog in which I was living my life. I spent a few months being a victim to what happened in my marriage. I realized that because I didn't know who I was, I didn't know how to set boundaries. I was not okay being alone. I had allowed this behavior to happen to me. I stayed and tried to work it out for seven years, but in my healing, I couldn't stay any longer.

In actuality, I'd spent those seven years preparing to take a leap of faith to leave my secure job and go back to graduate school to finish my studies in Counseling Psychology. I made the decision on my own without the approval or support of my spouse. It was both an exciting time and a challenging time. I was excited about where I was going, but I also had a person and circumstances in my life that I was allowing to hold me back. During the 20 years of being in relationship with Brian, we had established a deeply ingrained pattern of codependency. It was a horribly chaotic time for me as I started to practice healthy detachment. (I will cover codependency and healthy detachment later in the book.)

I had my breakthrough moment at home in Issaquah, Washington, while I was getting ready for graduate school to start. I was reading a book called *The Fifth Discipline* by Peter Senge. In it, Senge asked the reader to consider three questions:

Who are you?
Where are you going?
How will you get there?

These questions shook me to my core. I was 35 years old and I couldn't answer them. I had no clue who I was, where I was going, or how I was going, to get there. I realized that I had a lot of work to do to be able to honestly answer the questions. Between the ages of 35 and 41, I went through a process of reshaping my life.

Fast forward to the present and my life is completely different from how it was then. I revisited these three questions time and again. I worked through them until I could answer each one with clarity and confidence.

When it was time for me to start my practice as a psychotherapist, to help my clients, I turned to these powerful questions once more. I knew that my ultimate desire was to help my clients Accomplish Magnificent Things in their lives, but I wasn't sure how I would help them do so.

I sat down with a bottle of wine and my laptop one night to think about how I wanted to help people get unstuck. I asked myself, "What do I do with my clients? How do I help them see their beauty? How can I help them Accomplish Magnificent Things?" The answer didn't surprise me. It was all of my work related to the three questions that had confounded me several years earlier. Naturally, I would ask my clients to ask themselves those three powerful questions and I'd help them discover the answers. With my help and using the tools I created, my clients have been able to achieve incredible success and live the life of their dreams.

That's what I'm bringing to you in this book. I will be giving you all the tools I know. Not only do they work with my clients, they worked with me too. I want the same for you. The whole purpose of this book is to share what I've learned and help you work through these questions so you can know yourself better and live the life you truly desire.

For those of you who have enough courage to stick with me through the three sections of this book, you'll see how it unfolds. Together, we'll embark on a journey to answer these questions:

Who are you?
Where are you going?
How will you get there?

By exploring these questions in your life, and using the tools that I share with you, you'll be able to step forward confidently to Accomplish your own Magnificent Things!

Your life equation

If I could bottle life up in a condensed essence, what it comes down to is this: ultimately, your life is a sum of three parts. The first tool I want to share with you is best expressed as a mathematical equation:

Thoughts + Beliefs + Actions = Your Life

To take this equation a step further and to correlate them with my three questions, the equation also looks like this:

Who are you? = Your Thoughts
Where are you going? = Your Beliefs
How are you going to get there? = Your Actions

In this book you'll have a chance to explore your unique talents, gifts and way of thinking. You'll have an opportunity to examine your beliefs and get rid of limiting beliefs that are harming you. Lastly, you'll look at your past actions that have led you to where you are now, and be invited to choose different actions so you can create and live the life of your dreams.

I am honored that you have decided to go on this journey with me! Thank you!

So let's get started.

Who are you?

"Be who you were meant to be
and you will set the world on fire!"
—*St. Catherine of Sienna*

We're going to start this process of exploring who you are, using the Myers-Briggs Type Indicator (MBTI), to help you better understand yourself, as well as the important people in your life.

This is the best tool I have ever found to help us all understand our Innate selves (how we were born into this world). As I have said (and you will hear me say many times throughout this book), our Types do not change, only our life circumstances change. Every one of us is born with our Types, and then life circumstances either enhance or diminish that. In my experience, most of us get our Innate personality squished or suppressed out of us for any number of reasons, including:

- Abuse
- Birth order
- Culture of origin
- Demographics
- Poor educators
- Parents who didn't "get" us
- And many others

In my case, I had a very good, "normal" childhood, but I was a different Type than my mother and sister. Therefore, I always felt strange, misunderstood, and like a weirdo. I didn't understand why I saw the world differently than they did. It wasn't until high school when I met Mr. Sivertsen, my Leadership Development teacher who focused on personal development, that I felt accepted and normal for the first time in my life. He was a weirdo too, but he was a safe place for those of us that were the same Type as he was. We gathered together, worked on ourselves and learned about who we were. For that I will always be grateful to him. In fact, we are still friends today, because us weirdos need to stick together, you know?

Many of you reading this may not have had the chance to have a Mr. Sivertsen in your life, so this book might be the first exposure you have to truly understanding your innateness. If that is the case, you are in for a life changing experience, one I am so honored and grateful to share with you.

"Who are you?" has two parts:

1. **Nature**, which is how we are born into this world, our Innate personality Type and the core of this book. As Lady Gaga says, "Baby, I was born this way."

2. And **nurture**, our family of origin, birth order, culture of origin, traumas, our entire upbringing. It's all the stuff that our parents, classmates, teachers and other family did that influenced who we are today.

We don't live in a vacuum. What others do, say and how they behave impacts us positively and negatively. The words people say to us throughout the years get into our heads, our subconscious, and affect us greatly. In my experience, this "stuff" often turns into different forms of codependency, and it can rob us of living the life we were meant to live. In this book we are going to talk a lot about who we are innately and how we can build a life on that uniqueness. The number one thing that can hold us back from doing that is our codependent nature.

I realized I was codependent in my mid 30s. I was going through a rough patch with my husband and my therapist suggested I read *Codependent No More* by Melody Beattie. It was a life changing moment for me, and since that day I have considered myself a recovering codependent. I work on it each day because codependency is something that was ingrained in me during my childhood (nurture); therefore, I will always have the tendency to go back to that way of being.

Some of the learning in this book will be challenging for you, but I *know* that if you embrace it and accept the truth, it will change your life and your relationships forever. This will not happen overnight, but I hope this book will be a guide to you on your discovery of yourself—the good and the not so good.

I have chosen to start by discussing Type because understanding your personality Type is critical. It is the foundation of this book because personality Type is Innate and the basis of everything we are going to discuss from here on out. Personality Type is the very start of the process of coming to understand who we are. The reason I do this is because I know that understanding your own personality Type can help tremendously with:

- building awareness (and all change must start with awareness) of individual differences,

- enhancing your understanding of yourself and others

- appreciating the strengths and gifts of yourself and others

- knowing your own and others' personality Types, which provides you and others with a language and a framework for effective understanding and communication

Once we have uncovered your Innate personality Type using the MBTI basics, I will introduce my own unique way of incorporating it into your life; I call it "Living Your Life from the Front Seat." It is designed to help you understand your Type in a way that allows you to use it for the rest of your life, because I know it can and will change your life. It will help you understand yourself and your relationships in a new, powerful way. Get out a pen and a highlighter as you are going to want to take some notes as we move forward from here.

Buckle up, we are going to have some fun, and this stuff is going to rock your world.

Let's go!

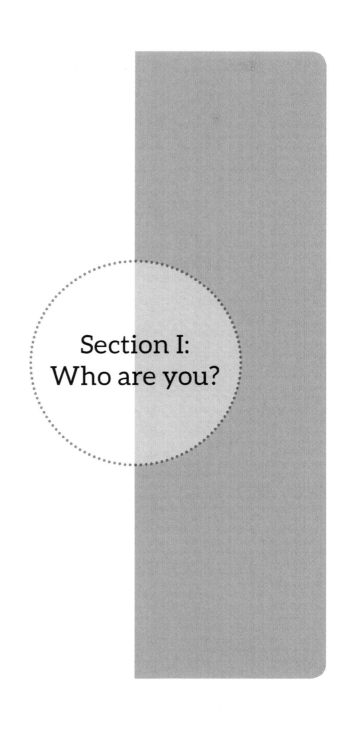

Section I:
Who are you?

Chapter 1

Myers-Briggs Type

"The thing that is really hard, and really amazing,
is giving up on being perfect and
beginning the work of becoming yourself."

—*Anna Quindlan*

I want you to imagine for a minute yourself as a child.

Who were you? What were you like? How did you interact with people? Were you funny and engaged with people? Or were you serious, and liked to come home from school and retreat to your room? Did you have imaginary friends? Have plays in your backyard? Or did you prefer to play alone and read?

I want you to take a moment in the space below and write down some thoughts, images or adjectives that you think describe you as a child.

_____

_____

_____

_____

_____

_____

_____

_____

_____

_____

_____

_____

_____

_____

_____

_____

What we are going to be doing over the following pages is to help you get back to that Innate child in you—who you were before the world got a hold of you and molded you into the person they thought you *should* be. My goal is to get you back to **you**!!

I want you to complete the following self-assessment as only you can. Let go of who you think your spouse wants you to be, or who your parents thought you should be, or what your job requires you to be.

But before you jump into the self-assessment, it is important for you to understand a little bit of background on Type. If you're an Intuitive Type like me, you might be tempted to jump past this seemingly boring stuff, but I promise it is important. Fortunately, one of my unique gifts is to take boring concepts and make them relatable and fun, so stick with me.

Background

There are some important foundational points to understand about Type; they are:

- understanding what Type is
- Type does not change, life circumstances change
- we have a preference
- there is a scale of preference

What is Type?

And where does it come from? We're first going to start by explaining Type: what it is and its origins. I know, I know, this is boring for you Intuitive Types, but I have made it short because it is important to understand. You sensing and thinking Types will love this.

The Myers-Briggs Type Indicator has its roots in the works of Carl Jung. Jung was a famous Swiss psychologist who talked about archetypes and how we understand ourselves through them. I say this somewhat jokingly, but I believe Jung must have been an NP (which you will learn more about) because he liked to start amazing projects, but moved on before he finished them.

In the 1940s, Isabella Myers and her daughter, Katharine Cook Briggs, took what Jung had described as archetypes and developed the Myers-Briggs Type Indicator. The MBTI has since become the most widely used personality assessment tool in the world. This is the most useful tool I have ever found to help people understand their innateness , and why I am spending my life teaching it and developing my own way of helping people understand it.

Type does not change

There is always someone who wants to arm-wrestle me over this topic, but personality Type is Innate; it does not change. Your life circumstances change, but your Type doesn't. **Let me say that again: your Type does not change, your life circumstances change.** While you may think that you were different in your youth than you are today, it wasn't your personality that changed—only your circumstances have changed.

Life circumstances are things such as our family of origin, our school or society. Each tells us that we're supposed to be a certain way, which may not enable our own strengths or Types. I will talk much more about that in the "Nurture" section.

Your Type does not change, your life circumstances change.

As children, we are who we are. We can be gregarious, or shy and reserved. We can be serious or playful. This is an example of our Innate nature. Until we are five to seven years old, we simply *are*. It's important, when you think about yourself as we work through this next section, to do your best to remember yourself as you were in your childhood. You want to get back to the person you were intended to be; the person that God/the Universe has created to bring your amazing gifts, talents and self to be a part of the world.

Over time, and through the influence of those around us,

we start to change—to try to fit into a certain mold. We try to work better within a society, within our families. Sometimes the roles that we are asked to take on are not ones where we feel strongest, happiest and healthiest. Many things enter our lives that change/conform us (school, parents, teachers, religious organizations).

You are meant to be a luminary, to shine light on this world, to share your God-given talents and to be sustained by them. If you have picked up this book, you're ready to bridge the gap between who you innately are and where you are now. I believe that you found this book because you are ready, now, to do this work. I want to get you back to who you are innately, so that you are living your best life for you and not for other people.

We have a preference
Handwriting example

Take a moment and do a little something for me in the space below. First, write your name with your dominant hand on the first line. How did that feel? Write down how that felt.

_____

_____

Now repeat this exercise on the first line of the second set of lines, with your non-dominant hand. Afterwards, write down (with whatever hand feels most comfortable) how that felt.

_____

_____

If you're like most people, when you wrote with your dominant hand it felt:

- comfortable

- natural

- easy

- confident

- strong

- second nature

- effortless

Alternately, when you wrote with your non-dominant hand, chances are you said that it felt:

- awkward

- sloppy

- challenging

- child-like

- uncomfortable

- like it took extra effort

I trust you are smart people (since you are reading this book), so you probably understand why I had you do this exercise. I did this because I wanted to illustrate a point. Everyone has a Type which is just like that handwriting exercise. Everyone is able to write with either hand, some to greater or lesser ability than others. Even if you're ambidextrous, one hand is still the one you prefer to work with over the other. The same holds for personality Type. While we may have a greater or lesser preference for doing things a certain way, we always have a preference.

If someone was to throw a ball at your face, you would try to catch it with your dominant hand 100% of the time; it would be second nature to you. Your Type preference is like this example—you *could* catch the ball and write your name with either hand, but you always have a preference for the dominate hand or your preferred Type.

Scale of preference
The teeter-totter

Imagine yourself standing on a teeter-totter. Standing in the middle, you have one foot on each side of the teeter-totter. As you imagine yourself walking to one side or the other, at some point, the end you're standing on is going to drop to the ground.

This is a visual of what it looks like to have a slight preference (in the middle) and a strong preference (way at one end).

- 1–5 is a slight preference
- 5–10 is a little stronger
- 10–20 is a clear preference
- 20–30 is a strong preference

In the middle of the teeter-totter, you are close to both sides of the spectrum, and therefore can understand both dichotomies and can also relate well to both. But as I stated in the section above about handwriting, you still always have a preference—even if it is slight.

As you move toward the seats, you are much farther away from the other side, and therefore don't relate as well to the other dichotomy.

Take a moment to close your eyes and imagine yourself on that teeter-totter. As we go through the self-assessment in the next section, imagine where you think you may fall on that scale of 1–30. Are you in the middle of the teeter-totter with a slight preference (1–5)? Or are you in middle with a clear preference (6–15)? Or are you at the end with a very strong preference (16–30)?

Something interesting can occur when we are looking at where we fall on the scale of preference in comparison to others in our lives. I have often seen an Extrovert think they can't be an Extrovert because in comparison to their spouse, partner or parent that is a strong Extrovert (25–30 on the scale), they assume they must be an Introvert. That is not true!

I have two clients this has happened to:

The first was a married couple where she was an extreme Type, 25–30 on every dichotomy. They had been married for 20 years, had their own business and four children. He had been functioning as her exact opposite Type, and they both assumed he was, until we Typed him. Lo and behold, he turned out to be the exact same Type as his wife, just not as strong as she was. Because she was so extreme in her preference, he assumed that he couldn't also be that Type, and had been taking on all the functions in the family as his opposite Type—and HATED it! He was exhausted, resentful, and sad. Since our work together, he has changed jobs, they have hired people to do the activities in their business that are in both of their Back Seats (I will explain this in more detail later) and they have so much more time and energy for each other, their business and their amazing kids.

The second example comes from an only child. She's a strong Extrovert, the strongest actually, a 30 out of 30. While I was typing her, she told me that she used to be an Introvert. I then explained that your Type does not change. I wondered what went on in her life as a little girl that may have made her not feel like she could show up as the innately strong Extrovert that she is. After a long pause and fighting back some tears, she told me that both her parents were actors and both strong Extroverts themselves. She felt that she could not shine as the strong Extrovert she was because both her parents already did that, so she retreated to her Back Seat of Introverted Thinking (again, I will explain these terms in more detail as we move forward).

Just because someone close to us is stronger on the scale doesn't mean we can't also be on that scale. It can certainly make us question ourselves, but this is not about comparing ourselves to others, this is just about us! So, as much as you possibly can, try to answer the self-assessment as you and only you, not in comparison to someone else in your life or family. OK?

There is no judgment in being who you are. You are who you are.

In this next section, we're going to use those teeter-totters to explore the different pairs of the Myers-Briggs Assessment tool – so that you can conduct your own self-assessment and figure out who you are. This will help you get to know who your best self is so that you can move forward in your life.

Don't put me in a box

There is always someone who says they don't like personality assessments because they don't like to be put into a box. Well, coming from someone who makes a living "thinking outside the box," I don't like that either, trust me!

I am no mathematician, but with four different dichotomies, a scale of preference from 1–30, and our nurtured selves (family of origin, birth order, traumas, culture of origin), no two people can be exactly alike. One Type is not going to look exactly like another Type, but they are similar, and it is just as important to understand how and why we are like some people and not like others. Myers-Briggs is the best tool I have ever found for that.

So, if you are one of those doubters and have gotten this far, please stick with me, you won't regret it. I will show you plenty of "outside of the box" thinking! I promise!

The MBTI is all about understanding who we are. Each dichotomy (set of opposite pairs) deals with different parts of our personality. There are four dichotomies: Extrovert/Introvert, Sensor/Intuitive, Thinking/Feeling and Judging/Perceiving. Each dichotomy deals with a separate part of our psyche. The **first** is all about energy—where you get your best energy. The **second** is how you take in information. The **third** is how you make decisions. The **fourth** is about how you like your world to be organized. Let's jump in and get started with this modified MBTI assessment, which will help you figure out who you are.

The dichotomies/pairings

I used to do a radio show with a colleague, where we talked each week about Type. She hated when I used the word dichotomies, and told me I needed to "dumb" it down and just use a word we all knew. We came up with pairing. While I was trained to use the word dichotomy, I realize many of you may have the same reaction she did, so I will use both words interchangeably.

The four pairings (or dichotomies) by Myers and Briggs are just the beginning of this amazing work, but an essential piece since everything builds on this foundation.

They are:

Extroversion and **I**ntroversion
Sensing and **IN**tuition[1]
Thinking and **F**eeling
Judging and **P**erceiving

The dichotomies are fascinating by themselves, but the work gets much deeper after we build this important foundation. Each can teach you so much about yourself and your relationships.

Typically, I am doing this work in person in a workshop setting, one-on-one with clients, or for a corporation. During this self-assessment someone always asks this important question, "But I am both, how do I choose?" My answer is, "You are both, but we always have a preference."

---

[1]*Myers and Briggs already used "I" for Introvert, so please notice that they use the letter N for Intuition*

As I said above, we always have a preference and it is going to be important to answer these sections from your most true self—who you are at your core. If you are starting this book rather lost or broken (as most of us are), this may take some time to flesh out and that is OK! I suggest going through this section with some self-compassion and honesty. Try not to answer these sections with who you *should* be or who your family *thinks* you should be or how your boss or spouse *wants* you to be, but who *you really are*!

This book is all about finding out who you are. As I shared with you in my story earlier, I was also lost, and it took me many years to get back to who I really am. Let this be the start for you. You can do it!

So, let's get started; it is going to be fun!

Chapter 2

Introversion and Extroversion

Most everyone has heard of Introverts and Extroverts, especially with the recent popularity of quirky Facebook and Pinterest posts about which Star Wars, Twilight or Downton Abbey character best fits your Type, along with Susan Cain's recent book, *Quiet* (about Introversion). However, this is often the most difficult pairing for people to choose from.

There is also some talk about Ambiverts, which is when someone feels they truly cannot choose between whether they have a preference for Introversion or Extroversion. While I appreciate this can be a difficult choice for many people, I think it's bullshit. You have to choose! It is important to know you have a preference, which you will learn more about later. Before we continue, I want to address a few concerns I hear about choosing between Introversion and Extroversion.

The main reason people have a difficult time choosing is because we evolve as we grow older. While we always have the same preference for either Extroversion or Introversion, the scale of our preference may change. As a child you most likely had a more extreme preference for either Introversion or Extroversion, but we live in the world with other people who influence our behavior (not our Type). Introverts may find themselves liking to be around people more as they age/evolve, or Extroverts may realize they may need more time alone, since they give so much of themselves to the world. Our preference has not changed, but the strength of it on the scale of 1–30 may become less severe. Up until my late 20s, I was a 28 on the scale of Extroversion; as I have grown older, I have simply learned to enjoy being alone. It doesn't mean I am now an Introvert. I am more like a 20 on the scale and I have learned to enjoy time by myself—journaling, traveling, reading and walking in nature. It brings me peace in my 40s that I couldn't experience in my 20s.

As we go along, I will be sharing my unique take on Type that I have curated over the past 20 years while working with clients. There are many books out there that are just about the facts of Type, but I find them rather boring and clinical (as I imagine many of you do as well). While I will share some facts, I have also broken down each section into unique areas that I hope will help you see each dichotomy in a new way to help you find your truest Type.

> *Extroversion and Introversion has to do with energy.*

Now, back to Extroversion and Introversion.

The first dichotomy has to do with energy—where you give your best energy and where you get your best energy. Introverts and Extroverts are energized in different ways, and people are either Extroverts (E) or Introverts (I), some to a greater extent than others (remember the teeter-totter), you can range from 1–30 on the scale.

Extroverts give their best energy to the world. They're energized by their outer world. They focus on people and things. They're typically pretty active. They have many interests, and often have many friends. Extroverts are external processors; they think aloud, verbally. There's no hidden best part of an Extrovert because they give that best self away to the world around them. Doing this energizes them and makes them happy.

Introverts, on the other hand, are energized by their inner world. They get energy and recharge from being alone. Introverts save their best self for themselves. They're focused on concepts and ideas, and are typically reflective. Introverts have few interests, but know them deeply. Likewise they have few friends, but a deep connection with those that they allow close to them. It takes time to get to know an Introvert and what is in their heart, as they show the world their second-best self, which we will dive into more in the next section.

Here are some common words to describe Introverts and Extroverts. Circle the words that you think best describe you.

Extrovert	Introvert
Energized by outer world	Energized by inner world
Focus on people, things	Focus on concepts, ideas
Active	Reflective
Lots of different interests	Depth of interest
Live it, then understand it	Understand it before live it
Outgoing	Inwardly directed

I have been working with Type for over 20 years. Through those years, I have come up with some unique ways to describe Type that help people really get it. I hope the following sections help solidify to you which you have a preference for, Introversion or Extroversion.

Where we give our best self

Imagine that you own a long-sleeve shirt with a heart painted on the sleeve. Think of the saying "wearing your heart on your sleeve." It relates to how some people show themselves and give themselves to the world.

Extroverts wear the heart facing out to the world. As you walk around the world, everyone can see the heart. In everything you do, you show people yourself. Your every gesture shows everyone who you are. Extroverts show and give their best self to the world. It is visible to the outside world just like the heart on the outside of your sleeve.

Introverts wear that shirt inside out. They wear the heart on the inside of their sleeve. The world does not see the Introvert's best self. They hide that best self and keep it for themselves. Someone has to get very close to you in order to see your true self, which is hiding on the inside of your sleeve. They need to get really close to be able to see what is truly inside of you.

With others

One of the biggest differences between Extroverts and Introverts is how they deal with people.

Introverts have a hard time in large groups; the small talk is tiring and difficult for them. They much prefer to have a one-on-one conversation, so they can go deeper with that one person. I have worked with countless Introverts that say small talk is literally painful for them. It isn't that they don't like or want to be social, but large parties or meetings where they are required to make small talk are not fun, nor something they are interested in doing.

Extroverts on the other hand get their energy from being with people, so they like "being on stage" at times. Being social and with others gives them energy, and since they are naturally good at it, they enjoy it.

External and internal processing

When I describe Introverts and Extroverts, I often talk about how these two Types process information. Each Type takes in information in their own way, and then processes it through different filters.

Extroverts are EXTERNAL processors.

Extroverts are EXTERNAL processors. They often talk before they think. They process information externally. Extroverts "live it, then understand it." When they are given new data or information, they will talk their way through it. If there is a problem in their life (or in someone else's life), Extroverts prefer to work things out in an external way. They might write an email, post something to Facebook or Tumblr or Instagram, draw something, dance or sing or do something physical to help them process the information they have gathered. They work through things outside of their heads. Whatever is easiest and closest, Extroverts tend to use it to work through their current issue/challenge.

Introverts are INTERNAL processors. They process information before they say it, write it, draw it or do anything with it. An Introverted person tends to be quiet, and to take in a lot of information before they are ready to form an opinion or make a decision and speak their mind. Because they take the time to process information before making a statement or contributing to a conversation, Introverts often go unheard in meetings. They often don't get a chance to add to the conversation and the decision making process, unless there are many other Introverts in the organization.

Extroverted world

The biggest challenge for Introverts is that, particularly in America, we live in a strongly Extroverted world. In America, Extroversion is rewarded. The child who is involved in a large variety of activities is perceived as being successful. They are the ones who are "running the world." So much of what we do is rewarded by what we are perceived to be doing. It's important for us to understand that Introverts need to process information differently than the other half of the population.

Introverts are INTERNAL processors.

If there is a meeting that is going to happen, the Extrovert is normally the one who is putting together the agenda, deciding who is going to do what, what is going to be discussed and running the meeting. They go from one point to another in rapid-fire sequence, not pausing to see if anyone has anything to add or ask at the time.

One of the things we need to learn about each other is that we take in information in different ways and at different speeds. Extroverts think and speak on the fly. Introverts need time to process information. Their filter is determining what they want to say at an appropriate time. This means that they need more time to get out their thoughts and feelings. What does that mean in our world today?

Extroverts sometimes need to stop talking to let the Introverts talk. Introverts need to find the courage to say, "I need to be heard." Knowing this can help us to communicate better in our relationships and businesses. If we don't take time to listen to Introverts, we're losing out on hearing from them. Externally processing doesn't make Extroverts more correct, it just makes them more vocal.

What others have to say

As you can well imagine, some character traits of one Type often cause stress for the other Type. When I recently ran a program with some clients, I divided the groups into their natural Types, and asked each Type (the Introverts and the Extroverts) several different questions including what they thought of the other Type, and what they wanted the other Type to know about them. The results of those discussions gave me a lot of insight into both Types.

What others have to say...

Extroverts about Introverts

When Extroverts were asked what they thought about Introverts, they said that they perceive Introverts as being:

- Selfish
- Hiding
- Quiet
- Shy
- Hard to know
- Individualistic
- Slow to communicate
- Needed for the little stuff
- All about them
- Have a dull life
- Rigid
- Mysterious
- Boring
- Easy to be alone
- Sensitive
- Pansies

- Thoughtful
- Dependable
- Reliable
- Loving
- Great listeners
- Inflexible
- Loyal
- Faithful
- Focused
- Careful
- Realistic
- Overthinking
- We are afraid you are lonely
- Want to shake you to know you are alive
- Slow

Introverts about Extroverts

On the other hand, when I asked Introverts what they thought about **Extroverts**, they said that they perceive **Extroverts** as being:

- Loud
- Pushy
- Bold
- Over
- whelming
- Impatient
- Impulsive
- Self-assured
- Playful
- More fun
- Unreserved

- Dismissive
- Obnoxious
- Too much
- Interesting
- Fascinating
- Exhausting
- Confident
- Powerful
- Unfiltered
- Squeaky wheel

Extroverts

During that same exercise at the workshop, I also asked each Type what they would like the other Type to know about them.

These answers were typical of what many **Extroverts** say that they want Introverts to know about them. **Extroverts** want you to know:

- We are exciting

- We want to know you

- We're outgoing

- We want to include you

- We're self-assured

- Forgive us for thinking out loud

- We really do want to hear you/include you

- We're expressive

- Our lack of filter isn't intended to hurt you

- We are loving, in a loud way

- We don't want to make you feel uncomfortable

- Our observations (like, "You're being quiet.") aren't meant to be critical—they are just our way of investigating or opening conversation

Introverts

I did the same exercise with the Introverts at a company retreat, and this group shared with me what **Introverts** want you to know about them:

- We are smart
- You are intimidating
- We need time alone, but don't exclude us
- Invite me to participate
- Listen to me when I talk
- Show me you get me
- Patience
- Quiet
- Time
- Compassion
- Interested in what we have to say
- Value in the way we do things
- Thoughtful = good
- Drop the timer
- Give me space to be my best
- Give me a chance to think and talk
- Understanding
- Respect
- Connection
- Just because I'm quiet doesn't mean I don't care, that I'm dumb or don't get it

Real stories

"Mary and David"

Clients of mine, who we will call Mary and David, came to see me last year because they were struggling to communicate, a trait shared by many of my clients. We did some initial work to assess what the issues were and get over some major humps. Then we did their personality assessments and the "aha's" started to happen! David is a strong Extrovert. He likes to be around people, and he gets his energy from spending time with friends, talking, going out, being in nature, happy hour and talking with his wife. Mary, a strong Introvert, liked being alone a majority of the time. She enjoyed silence and solitude after a long day at work. She could simply be in the same room with David and feel connected even though they were just watching TV, reading together or on their own computers. She felt connected and felt like they were spending quality time together. As we started to talk through this, David realized that he did not have those same feelings—he felt isolated from Mary, often wondered what she was thinking and wished they could be out doing something. We spent a few weeks talking about their differences in just this one area and how they could navigate them together and compromise so that they both were getting their needs met within, and outside of, the relationship.

David felt guilty leaving Mary alone, which we soon realized was all made up in his head. Mary did not mind being left alone one or two nights a week to do her own

Introverted things like reading, taking a bath and doing research online for things she liked. David started doing things with friends a few nights a week to fulfill his need for interaction and activity.

They also started compromising on the things they did together on date nights. Mary was happy staying home, while David always wanted to go out. So, while neither loved the other's plans, they did so happily knowing and understanding (for the first time ever) the importance of their differences and how they could make each other happy.

It was certainly a relationship-changing realization for Mary and David. Knowing and understanding their differences gave them language and a framework to start using so they could express their needs without hurting one another.

"Samantha and Greg"

I had another couple recently, we will call them Samantha and Greg, where she was the Extrovert and he was the Introvert. Unlike Mary and David, Samantha and Greg were in real crisis when they came to see me. Samantha spent most of her time yelling at Greg trying to get him to pay attention to her in any way possible. She was constantly externally processing, mostly in harsh, negative ways. Greg was a very strong Introvert, (a 30 out of 30), and almost all of his thoughts were internally processed for a long time before they came out of his mouth. In our sessions together, Samantha and I would need to sit quietly for long periods of time waiting for Greg to speak, but when he did, it was vulnerable, real, loving and quite profound. He needed time to process his thoughts and feelings. Samantha had to learn to shut up and give Greg time to process, and realize his silence didn't mean he was not engaged. It simply meant he needed time to determine what he wanted and needed to say. It was work for both of them, but the end result was a profoundly deeper understanding for one another. While frustrating at times, they were able to navigate through it once they had the understanding of their differences and some tools to work through them.

Which one are you?
Extrovert or Introvert?

So, I have given you as much detail as I can to hopefully give you confidence to choose which one you have a preference for and to what degree: (1–30). So, take a moment here and choose which one best describes you. Where do you think you fit on the Extrovert/Introvert scale? Are you strongly Introverted? Are you strongly Extroverted? Or are you somewhere in between? Draw yourself where you think you are on that teeter-totter.

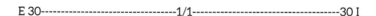

E 30--------------------------------1/1--------------------------------------30 I

Chapter 3

Sensing and Intuition

This is my favorite pairing because it has defined my entire life. Once you hear more about it, you may feel the same way.

As I mentioned in *Letter to my readers* and my *Introduction*, I have always felt like a weirdo. I have always thought different, felt different and wanted more. It took me many years to realize that this part of my personality is the reason why I have always had these feelings. I now work almost exclusively with Intuitive Types to help them realize that their differences from the majority of the population are *not* a bad thing, but part of what makes them unique and special.

Sensing (S) and Intuition (N) is about how we take in information.

In this section, I will explain the huge differences in this dichotomy and how you can learn to understand them and embrace them, whether you are Sensing or Intuitive.

Most people are not aware of how much this part of our innate personality affects our lives, our relationships, and how we feel about ourselves. Most everyone has heard about Extroversion and Introversion, but few people know about Sensing and Intuition, and how important they are to understanding ourselves and our relationships. There is also a huge discrepancy in the division of people in this dichotomy, which I will talk about much more.

The dichotomy of Sensing (S) and Intuition (N) is about how we take in information. Some people take in information through their five senses—we call these people Sensors, and they are represented by the letter S. Others are Intuitive, represented by the letter N, and go more by gut and energy rather than facts.

Sensors validate information via their five senses.

Sensors validate information via their five senses. Information is valid if they can touch it, taste it, hear it, smell it or see it. Sensors are very literal, concrete and factual. I call Sensors the "internal file cabinet." In their brains, they remember how someone looked at them, the tone in their voice or if they rolled their eyes at them. Sensors live in the here and the now. They are happiest now, and aren't always looking to what's next. Strong Sensors are big on routine, and the nine to five. They tend to take things literally and live in the moment. And, Sensors make up 75% of the world's population! Yes, 75 percent. They are "gotten" by most people since 3/4 of the population are like them. Sensors are a huge part of the muggle world that is described in the *Harry Potter* books. Most people are Sensing Types, and therefore they can relate to one another easier.

Intuitive Types take in information via their "sixth" sense.

Intuitives (N), the other 25% of the world's population, are what I call future-thinkers and "what-if'ers." Where Sensors take in information with their five senses, Intuitive Types take in information via their "sixth" sense. Intuitive Types have an energetic vibe, gut feeling, a hunch or a speculation about someone or something. Intuitive Types are more figurative than literal. Intuitive Types prefer the big picture. They walk into a room and immediately get a vibe for what is going on. They just have a sense of something, so it's less specific and bigger picture. Intuitive Types often think about what's next, need to dream and spend a lot of time imagining what could come next.

Here are a few key words to describe each Type. Which words resonate with you? Circle the words that feel best to you.

Sensing	Intuition
Facts	Meanings
Data	Possibilities
Detail	Hunches, speculation, gut instinct
Reality-based	
Here and now	Theoretical
Literal	Fantasy
	Figurative

Weirdos and the muggle world

As I mentioned earlier, there is a huge discrepancy in population breakdown between Sensing and Intuitive Types. It warrants repeating that sensors make up 75% of the population and Intuitive Types make up the other 25 percent.

I am confident that most of you reading this book are the weirdos—Intutive Types. Why do I know this? Because I am one as well, and I know our Type *very* well. We love personal development, we are always looking for the next greatest thing to learn about ourselves, we are never done learning, we are always striving for more, more, more. Intuitives are drawn to this book for the same reason I am writing it—we have a desire for more knowledge, more growth, more personal development and more evolving.

This is not to say that all Sensing Types don't want this as well, but they are simply better at just "being," which most Intuitive Types envy. I have often said being an Intuitive Type is a blessing and a curse. While we love being creative and learning, it can be exhausting to rarely be satisfied with what is. While Sensors have an ability to just be, Intuitives are always thinking about what's next, and that can be exhausting.

Sensors have an amazing ability to deal with the day-to-day world that Intuitives have a hard time with. As 75% of the population, the world is designed more for them. We Intuitive Types are a little weird. Am I right? Have you always felt a little different? Misunderstood? Me, too.

Please remember, there is no right or wrong Type. I am simply calling it like it is, and in doing so, I hope that it resonates with you more than if you had heard it in the past. My intention in being a little sassy and honest is so you will get it and start using it. As I have mentioned, understanding this and implementing it will change your life for the better.

Alliance and the Hoard

A client taught me about World of Warcraft. I have never played it, but for those of you that have, you will get this. She compared Sensing Types to the "Alliance" and Intuitive Types to the "Hoard." My understanding is that the Alliance is the muggle world—they are the responsible people in the world, the 9–5'ers, the "normal" ones. The Hoard are the weirdos, the woo-woo people, the creative Types.

Small talk

Small talk to Intuitive Types can be exhausting. They want to talk about concepts, big picture ideas, they are curious and enjoy deep conversations about theories and possibilities. Small talk at parties can seem frivolous and a waste of time—especially for Introverted Intuitive Types.

Sensors are much better at talking about details and facts that often come from small talk with co-workers or at parties.

Internal file cabinet

Sensors have an internal file cabinet in their brains where they store details about people, places and things they can recall years later! If someone rolled their eyes at them back in 1995, they have that stored in their memory banks for later and pull it out to use when necessary.

Sensors are also quite traditional when it comes to holidays, birthdays and other special occasions. This also has to do with their "file cabinet" of a brain. They have experienced special occasions a certain way in the past and they prefer things to stay that way.

Funnel

Imagine a funnel. Intuitive Types take in information and live at the top of the funnel—big picture, big concepts, ideas; lots of space to dream, to think, to create future ideas. There is more space at the top of the funnel.

Sensors take in information and like to live at the bottom of the funnel—details, specifics, concrete ideas, here and now, more compact ideas.

Money is a great example of this funnel. Intuitive Types typically know they have enough money, but not usually the exact amount, whereas Sensing Types want to know EXACTLY how much money they have. Big picture vs. details. If you think you are an Intuitive Type but you are always worried about exactly how much money you have, you are likely living your life in the Back Seat, which we will talk about in great detail in the following sections.

Here and now vs. future

This is one of the most important differences between Sensing and Intuitive Types. I have touched on it, but want to spend a little more time on it here.

Intuitive Types are always thinking about the future and what's next. I call them "what-if'ers."

You will hear them say things like, "Honey, *what if* we moved the kids to Costa Rica for a year and sold coconuts on the beach? *What if* we went to Iceland this year? *What if* I quit my job and wrote a book? *What if* we move abroad for a year and let the kids experience other cultures? What if, what if, what if...?" Intuitive Types are also dreamers; they love to dream and play with all possibilities. Sometimes Ns don't even have to act on all of their dreams, but they still like to dream. It is actually essential to them. It is part of their makeup.

As I have mentioned before, Intuitives have a hard time living in the moment. They are always thinking about what's next. Whether that be dinner, the next trip, the next big family event—anything really. Their minds are almost always there and not here. Again, I call this a blessing and a curse as I love the dreamer in me. But it also doesn't fit in with the muggle world. I find myself extremely disappointed at times when things or people don't live up to my expectations.

Sensors are in the moment most of the time. They live in the here and now, and have an ability to simply "be" that Intuitives do not.

These differences can of course cause many issues in relationships between Sensors and Intuitives. I share a few in the *Real stories* section to come. You may find yourself resonating with them, which can help you determine your own Type.

Walking into a room

When walking into a room, Sensing and Intuitive Types will take in information differently.

Intuitive Types immediately get a sense of the energy of the room. They notice how the room looks, the lighting, the music, the energy of the people there. They take in the overall energy to make their decisions about it.

Sensing Types scan the room for details: who is there, how people are standing, how someone looks at them when they enter the room, how people are dressed and their body language. Specific, detailed information that helps them understand the environment they just walked into in a way they can process. All that information goes into the file cabinet in their brain so they can use it later to make decisions or use their intuition with people. Yes, Sensing Types still have intuition, they just use it differently than Intuitive Types.

The word "intuition" seems to imply that Sensors don't have it, and that isn't the case. While Sensors don't always read energy the way that Intuitives can, they can have intuition, sometimes very strong intuition. Since Sensors take in *Sensing doesn't mean you don't have intuition.* information via their five senses, they use that to read situations to get an intuitive hit. They scan their environment (or a person) for specific cues to give them data for their intuition. They read body language, the environment, tone of voice and eye movement.

I had a budding therapist reach out to me a few years ago. After learning her personality Type was Sensing, she believed that she would be a horrible therapist since she didn't have intuition. After talking for an hour or so, she realized she did in fact have a strong intuition with her clients and in her life. She just took it in via her excellent skills of observation.

So, you Sensors out there, don't fret. You can develop and rely on your intuition as part of your life.

Sensors about Intuitives

When Sensors were asked what they thought about **Intuitives**, they said that they perceived **Intuitives** as being:

- Flakey
- Head in the clouds
- Goofy
- Not sensible
- Never present
- Always thinking about what's next
- Unhappy unless planning a trip
- Creative
- Artsy
- Different
- Has a good gut feeling for people

Intuitives about Sensors

On the other hand, when I asked Intuitives what they thought about **Sensors**, they said that they perceive **Sensors** as being:

- Rigid
- Controlling
- Boring
- Too detail oriented
- Needs to learn to go with the flow
- Good at day-to day life stuff
- Better with money than themselves
- Dream killers
- Would like them to think outside the box

"What I want you to know about me"

Sensors

During that same exercise, I also asked **Sensors** what they want Intuitive Types to know about them. These answers are what **Sensors** say they want you to know about them:

- We need details
- We need you to be specific
- We can be intuitive too, we just do it differently than you
- Respect my need for specifics
- I remember every eye roll
- Words are powerful to me, choose them carefully

Intuitives

What **Intuitives** want you to know about them:

- We need to be able to dream, let us

- We may or may not follow through on all our ideas, but we still like to have them and share them with you

- We are smart

- We don't always have details for you, we trust our gut

- Details and facts are hard for us

- Dreaming is more fun than day-to-day

- Just because we are always thinking about the future doesn't mean we don't like our lives

- We need to be creative

Real stories
"Nicole and Roger"

I had a couple come to me a few years ago that was seemingly quite in love with one another. As they started the session, they were affectionate and sweet with each another. I was curious to learn what issues would present themselves in our first session. Roger, as it turns out, was a strong Intuitive Type (30), and Nicole was a strong Sensing Type (27). Their issue, unbeknownst to them, revolved around this difference in their personality Types.

Nicole started by telling me how she felt Roger didn't love her and their two children. He always seemed to be dreaming of the next best thing and never present in their day-to-day life. Roger talked often in their marriage about taking trips around the world with the kids, quitting their jobs and moving to Maui and getting simple jobs so they could eliminate some stress in their lives. Nicole viewed that as Roger wanting to run away from their life together and the children. But, Roger wanted to do it *together*. Over the years, this began to create distrust and space between them. Once we discussed their Types and they realized that they both loved each other very much and wanted nothing more than to be together, we could talk openly about the differences between their innate personalities and work on some ways they could both be happy.

They worked out an agreement that during the week was day-to-day life, but on Wednesdays, Roger was able to go do something out of the box. They started traveling more as a family, which gave Roger something to research, plan for, and look forward to. Nicole was able to *hear* Roger now that her feelings weren't being hurt by thinking he was unhappy in the marriage.

"Brian and I"

My ex-husband and I are still good friends. While we were talking about me getting close to finishing this book, a perfect example of the difference between his Sensing Type and my Intuitive Type came up.

I was telling him about how I wanted the book to look: the images, the quotes and the overall feel of the book. He looked at me rather blankly and simply said, "Won't that take away from the margins?" I laughed. Yes, he was right—and I don't give a shit. Also, he was right when he pointed out that I will not make as much on the sale of each book because it will cost me more to produce it this way. But, the way this book looks is the vision I had for it, and I know that the majority of you reading this right now appreciate it very much. The book's layout is part of the experience for the reader, and it is important to me as an Intuitive Type. It is about more than just the words you are reading right now. The overall feel, color and your experience of the book are important to me. I know you Intuitive Types *get* this and you Sensing Types are thinking the exact same thing Brian was. It is OK. We are just different and that is awesome!

Which one are you?
Sensing or Intuition?

I have given you as much detail as I can to hopefully give you confidence to choose which one you have a preference for and to what degree: (1–30). So, take a moment here and choose which one best describes you. Where do you think you fit on the Sensing and Intuition scale? Are you strongly Sensing? Are you strongly Intuitive? Or are you somewhere in between? Mark yourself where you think you are on the scale.

S 30-------------------------1/1------------------------30 N

Chapter 4

Thinking and Feeling

As you can likely tell by now, I am intrigued by marginalized Types, and this dichotomy carries with it two different marginalized Types, thinking women and feeling men.

This is the only dichotomy that is affected by gender, and it is also largely influenced by society. Roughly 75% of men are Thinkers and roughly 75% of women are Feelers.

The Thinking and Feeling dichotomy has to do with how we make decisions.

The Thinking and Feeling dichotomy has to do with how we make decisions. The MBTI uses the letter T for Thinking and F for Feeling. Once we've taken in our information through either Sensing or Intuition, we have to make decisions based on that.

Thinkers make decisions with their heads. They like analysis. They like facts. They're objective and logical decision makers. This makes many Thinkers seem impersonal when it comes to decision making. It's not that they don't care about people, it's that they carefully analyze the pros and cons and make decisions that meet their criteria.

Feelers, on the other hand, primarily make decisions with their feelings. They also include everybody else's feelings that could be affected by their choice. Each decision is made depending on the circumstances. This can cause a lot of conflict between individuals who make decisions in different ways, whether in an intimate relationship or at work.

What's interesting is the challenge that male Feelers and female Thinkers experience in dealing with people who are the typical gender/Type association in this personality Type. Women who are Thinkers are often seen and categorized as bitches, and men who are Feelers are often seen and categorized as weak and indecisive. There is no judgment in being who you are. Simply accept that this is who you are, and learn how to work with others who are different than you.

Thinking	Feeling
Analysis	Sympathy
Objective	Subjective
Logic	Humane
Impersonal	Personal
Criteria	Circumstances

The other 25%

With roughly 75% of women as Feelers and roughly 75% of men as Thinkers, that leaves only 25% of women as Thinkers and 25% of men as Feelers.

As with Intuitive Types, living your life as only 25% of the population can leave people feeling left out, misunderstood, marginalized and as if they are on the outside looking in.

I enjoy working with marginalized Types, and I find many of my female clients are Thinkers and many of my male clients are Feelers. Why? Because they have spent most of their life feeling left out and not knowing why, until I explain Type to them. As we explore Type together, they start to understand these feelings of being different and left out. They can start to appreciate their uniqueness and rareness in this world.

Thinking women report feeling left out when around other women. They don't feel "gotten." They would rather spend time with men, and often find they have more male friends than they do female friends. Oftentimes when other women are sharing their feelings, it can make them feel uncomfortable and awkward.

Feeling men report similar experiences of feeling left out or misunderstood. They often don't "get" other men and other men don't "get" them. They prefer to have deeper relationships with women where they feel free to talk about their feelings.

Society plays a role

Society tells little girls they are *supposed* to be sweet and sensitive, want to sit around and talk about their feelings and care about how everyone is feeling. But what if you don't? When you are born a Thinking woman, you likely felt a little different from an early age. You may have wanted to go play with the boys instead of playing house with the other little girls. As you can imagine, this can be quite confusing for little girls, and likely this has stuck around into adulthood.

Also, society tells men they are *supposed* to be tough, make difficult decisions and not cry. But what if you do cry, are sensitive and make decisions with your feelings as a man? Just like Thinking women, Feeling men feel different and left out. They grow up wondering if something is wrong with them.

I am going to share two powerful stories in the *Real stories* section about a Thinking woman and a Feeling man so you can get a better sense of what this feels like for these marginalized Types. My intention is for us to have a greater understanding of ourselves and others so we can stop labeling people as bitches or softies, and simply understand we are all just born different and learn how to navigate relationships with all the different kinds of people in this world.

Opposites attract

It has been my experience that opposites truly do attract. I have no real statistics on this, it is just my clinical observation over the years.

It is probably not surprising that in most heterosexual relationships, just based on statistics, that most Feeling women are partnered with Thinking men.

However, I have found it fascinating that in the hundreds of couples I have worked with over the years, most Thinking women are partnered with Feeling men. And in most homosexual relationships, one partner is Feeling and other is Thinking.

This concept of "opposites attract" goes back to caveman days when we needed a nurturing partner (woman) to care for the children and the relationships of the clan. And we needed a practical provider (man) to take care of the survival needs and status of the family. We seem to not have evolved as much as we might have thought!

Thinkers about Feelers

When Thinkers were asked what they thought about **Feelers**, they said that they perceived **Feelers** as being:

- Flakey
- Too emotional
- Talks too much
- Overly sensitive
- Shares too many feelings
- Can appear silly

Feelers about Thinkers

On the other hand, when I asked Feelers what they thought about **Thinkers**, they said that they perceive **Thinkers** as being:

- Harsh
- Impersonal
- Without feelings
- Better decision makers
- Curt
- Short
- Too critical
- Uncaring
- Insensitive

"What I want you to know about me"
Thinkers

I also asked **Thinkers** what they want Feeling Types to know about them. These answers are what **Thinkers** say that they want you to know about them:

- We have feelings
- We care
- We just make decisions with facts
- We need you to be a little more logical at times

"What I want you to know about me"
Feelers

What **Feelers** want you to know about them:

- We have a lot of feelings, about most everything
- Other people's opinions of us matter
- We value feelings
- Just because we make decisions with our hearts doesn't mean we aren't smart
- Value our feelings
- Ask us how we feel about things
- Our feelings aren't always logical and that needs to be OK

Real stories
Feeling man – "James"

James came to me quite a few years ago—broken, sad and on the verge of being suicidal. He had spent his 35 years on this earth feeling different from all other men. He questioned his sexuality, his identity and his manhood. After talking for a long time and hearing how much of his life revolved around typical "Thinking male" activities, we examined his Type and discovered he was an extreme Feeling man, (29 out of 30). As we talked about what it meant to be a Feeling man, how it felt, and the things he experienced as simply part of his Type, he started to cry. For the first time in his life, he was seeing and understanding why he had felt different all these years. He knew from that moment on he needed to start embracing his Feeling side and likely needed to make some changes in his life. He was also able to cultivate this for his son who was also a Feeler. I can happily report he is doing well and living much more of his life from the Front Seat.

Thinking woman – "Kathy"

Kathy, a female business owner, hired me a few years ago to coach her around her business. She knew she had a brilliant business idea, which she did, but it just wasn't taking off and she couldn't figure out why. Her product was made exclusively for women, which meant she needed to connect and sell to women. As we Typed her in my office, we quickly realized she was an ENTJ, a strong thinking woman (28 out of 30). The light bulbs started to go off for her. She realized that the reason she was having a hard time selling her business idea to women is because she doesn't really connect to the majority (75%) of women. Her somewhat abrasive style was not attractive to most women. She is a brilliant idea woman, and is excellent at making things happen (her Front Seat), but she needed a Feeling saleswoman to help her connect with her ideal clients. She did just that and her business has been growing ever since. And, she gets to focus on the things she is great at.

Thinking and Feeling couple - "Monica and Carrie"

This could be 90% of the couples I have worked with over the years, but one in particular comes to mind. And it is actually a same sex couple; we will call them Monica and Carrie. Monica is a strong Feeler, (26 out of 30) and Carrie is a strong Thinker, (21 out of 30). Feeling Monica often reports a lack of emotional support by Carrie, which makes her feel managed or controlled. Thinking Carrie reports that Monica is over-emotional and never knows what to say to her to comfort her in times of need. When we Typed them, they were not surprised by the results, and also felt some relief that there was a reason and some language to use to help them communicate to one another. While this still continues to be a struggle in their relationship (as it does in many other Thinking/Feeling partnerships), they have a new understanding to help them navigate the other's ways of making decisions and seeing the world.

Which one are you?
Thinking or Feeling?

I have given you as much detail as I can to hopefully give you confidence to choose which one you have a preference for and to what degree: (1–30). So, take a moment and choose which one best describes you. Where do you think you fit on the Thinking and Feeling scale? Are you strongly Thinking? Are you strongly Feeling? Or are you somewhere in between? Draw yourself where you think you are on the scale.

30--------------------------1/1--------------------------30 F

Chapter 5

Judging and Perceiving

The last dichotomy in the MBTI is Judging (J)/Perceiving (P). This has to do with how you like your world organized and how you like to be organized in the world. This is often the root cause of a lot of angst in a relationship.

> *Judging (J)/Perceiving (P). This has to do with how you like your world organized and how you like to be organized in the world*

All the dichotomies are my favorite for different reasons:

- E/I because it helps clarify so much about communication

- S/N because it is such a huge factor in so many Intuitives' lives to help them understand their differences in this world

- T/F because the other 25% fascinate and intrigue me as they often feel misunderstood and left out

- but this last one, J/P, because it is funny and I like funny

I want to start this section with what I call it "The Boat Story".

I had the divine pleasure of sailing the British Virgin Islands with my ex-husband and some friends many years ago. While on the boat, I quickly realized I was one of only two Judgers. The other eight people on the boat were Perceivers.

I got up the first morning on the boat and went upstairs with everyone else to start our beautiful morning with coffee and breakfast. Before I could take my first sip of coffee, the J in me started asking all the normal J questions:

- What are we having for breakfast?
- What time is breakfast?
- Where are we going today?
- What islands will we be snorkeling at?
- Can you show me on a map?
- Where are we having lunch?
- What are we having for lunch?
- What are we doing after lunch?
- Are we getting off the boat today?
- If so, which island?
- What's fun on that island?
- Where are we having dinner?
- What time does the sun set?

I felt great and complete with the plan for the day. I could now relax into my day knowing the plan. Filled with contentment, I looked over at my friends and their mouths had dropped to the floor in shock and horror as I had just ruined their day! Part of the fun of Ps, especially in an environment like a catamaran in the BVIs, is to let the day unfold as it comes. They wanted things to be spontaneous and to have *no* plan.

It was such a hilarious and poignant moment in my life, that I tell this story at almost every workshop, because each Type always has such an intense reaction. Js agree with me whole heartedly and Ps usually look at me with disgust as I am telling this story. You may have had a similar response reading this.

The next morning I still *needed* to know the plan but didn't want to ruin it for my P friends. I took the captain aside and asked all the same questions, but only *I* knew the plan for the day. Great lesson of compromise!

Judgers like things organized. Judgers like to be on time and settled and planned and decisive. They like to control their life and—let's get really honest—they like to control other people's lives too, because if you're not in line with a J's life, you're kind of messing it up. Judgers have a calendar and agenda and use them religiously. They like to create lists (and most importantly, they like to check things off their list). If you invite a Judger to a last-minute get together, chances are they're already booked or they might not want to come because it's so unexpected.

Perceiving people are flexible and spontaneous. They go with the flow and let life happen. Perceiving people are undaunted by surprise and enjoy the opportunity to do something flying by the seat of their pants. They don't tend to make plans too far in advance because they don't know if they'll be available. If something else that interests them more than what you have planned comes along, they might just opt to do something else.

Judging	Perceiving
Organized	Pending
Settled	Flexible
Planned	Spontaneous
Decisive	Tentative
Control one's life	Let life happen
Set goals	Undaunted by surprise

Confusing J and P with S and N

There is very often confusion with the second (Sensing and Intuition) and the last (Judging and Perceiving) dichotomies. While I am typing someone in a workshop, corporate retreat or one on one, when we are discussing Sensing and Intuition there is some confusion with how it correlates to Judging and Perceiving. Often Intuitive Types think they must be a Judger because they are always thinking about the future, but nothing could be further from the truth. You can very much be an Intuitive Type and also a Perceiver; they are completely separate. Again, **Sensing** and **Intuition has to do with how we take in information** and the **Judging and Perceiving dichotomy has to do with how we like to be organized in this world and how we like our world organized.** You can still take in information via your intuition and always be thinking about what is next, but also like to be less structured and spontaneous, flitting from one thing to the next, like most NPs.

I hope you can start to see how each pairing plays a very special role in and of itself. In the next couple of sections, we are going to start pairing the dichotomies together to really have some fun and see them in a whole new way that will give you even deeper understanding.

Work and play or work then play

Judgers like to work *then* play, meaning, they don't like to mix things, while Perceivers like to work *and* play, and can do both at the same time.

Imagine yourself at the office or the PTA, and a meeting is about to start. Before the meeting begins, Judgers and Perceivers are likely to be small talking. Even as the meeting starts there may be a little personal catching up going on, but at some point the Js will want the small talk to stop and the meeting to begin while Ps would prefer to continue with the fun, personal talk through the meeting. Ps can mix business and pleasure while Js prefer them to be separate.

I told you this was funny! Can you see yourself and others more clearly in the dichotomy now?

How will you take this information and use it in your life, your relationships and your business?

Don't worry about it, we'll figure it out

"Don't worry about it, we'll figure it out." Don't EVER say this to a J!

While Ps like to go with the flow, figure things out as they go and assume everything will work out (and that is a great mentality to have), this stresses Js out and actually causes them anxiety.

I have worked with countless parents and their children over the years on this. P parents with J kids need to be aware that their "go with the flow" attitude does not work for their J kids that need to have a plan, need to have structure and need to know what is going on. Children (and adults, for that matter) can show signs of anxiety and often think they need to be put on medication, but sometimes these J kids just need some structure in their lives.

I often think about the first day of school when it comes to this dichotomy. As a strong J, I used to worry for weeks about the first day of school. I would have nightmares about not knowing how to get to my classes or forgetting where my locker was. My mom would take me to school as soon as I received my schedule. We would walk the halls so I could map out where everything was and where I needed to be. Do this for your J kids—they need it. Often parents assume their children are just being difficult, but J kids— really just need to know what is going on so they can relax and enjoy the rest of their summer or their day. This example really goes for anything—a typical Saturday or a vacation or a visit from a relative. In order for a J to relax and be back in the present moment, they need to know the plan.

Js and Ps as parents

This dichotomy/pairing can be challenging for parents.

Innate J moms or dads who typically like structure learn very quickly that they have to learn to go with the flow now that they are parents.

And Innate P moms or dads who typically like to go with the flow learn very quickly they have to learn to keep some sort of schedule or things fall through the cracks.

We all have things in our lives that we simply have to do. Learning who you are innately is important so that when you have to do the things you don't really like to do, you can understand that it stretches you in ways that are going to cause you stress and you won't be at your best.

A parent who is a P may have to keep some sort of schedule, but they are at their best when they are simply playing and being spontaneous with their kids. And a J parent has to learn to go with the flow at times, but they are at their best when they can keep a clear schedule and keep on track.

I want you to choose all of these dichotomies based on who you are. Not you as a parent, as an employee, as a son, daughter, brother, or sister. But you, innately. Can you promise to do that?

Judging world

While the Judging/Perceiving split is almost 50/50, we live in a world today where being driven, over planned, and organized is rewarded. We see it everywhere from stay-at-home moms being overscheduled, to Corporate America's endless meetings, to even children being pushed to the brink with hours of homework while somehow maintaining sports and other after school activities.

We live in a cell phone, "everything at your fingertips" generation, and this can be exhausting and overwhelming for everyone, but especially P Types. They are wired to need "no plans, no structure, let life happen" and they get very little of that in today's overscheduled life. I see so many men and women in my practice who are at their wits' end trying to juggle the demands of life: working, raising children, taking vacations. They are burned out!

It is true that Js can handle the structure of today's world a bit better than Ps. Again, no judgment, remember? Ps need a break sometimes, possibly every week where they have a day they can do whatever strikes them in the moment. It isn't being lazy or irresponsible, it is simply who they are.

I do this work because I want more acceptance for who we innately are and for us to quit "pathologizing" each other. How much easier would your life be if you were allowed to be who you innately are more of the time? And how much better would your relationships be if you loved your partner, for who they are and quit trying to make them be who you want them to be? Learn this stuff. It will change your life and your relationships, I promise.

At this point, if you are reading this alone (and you are in a relationship) get another copy and give it to your partner, because understanding all of this can change your life and your relationships. I hope you are seeing that.

Judgers about Perceivers

When Judgers were asked what they thought about **Perceivers**, they said that they saw **Perceivers** as being:

- Flakey
- Unorganized
- Late
- Lazy
- Irritating
- Fun
- Spontaneous
- Wished they could be more like them
- Go with the flow

Perceivers about Judgers

On the other hand, when I asked Perceivers what they thought about **Judgers**, they said that they see **Judgers** as being:

- Rigid
- Controlling
- Uptight
- Annoying
- Organized
- Wished they could be more like them
- Scheduled
- Need to be able to let go

Judgers

During that same exercise in my workshops, I also asked **Judgers** what they want Perceiver Types to know about them. **Judgers** want you to know:

- They are fun
- They need to know the plan in order to relax
- Don't ever say to them "don't worry about it, we will figure it out"—it stresses them out more
- They need a plan
- Your "no plan" attitude stresses them out
- Help by keeping somewhat of a weekly planner as a team or a family
- When you are late they find it rude and disrespectful

"What I want you to know about me"

Perceivers

- Your plans stress them out
- They need to have a day a week to just be, with no plans
- They aren't flakey, it is just the way they like to be

Real stories
"Karen and John"

Karen and John were a newly dating couple that came into my office and showed classic signs of the J and P dichotomy. Karen a very strong J, (30 out of 30), reported that John's lack of planning for their future together made her feel unimportant to him. He said he was in love with her and wanted to be with her, but he couldn't make plans for the following weekend, let alone plans for them to start a life together. John, a strong P, (23 out of 30), reported feeling managed and controlled by Karen because of her obsessive need to know what was happening at all times. He wanted her to just see how the relationship would naturally unfold and to try to live in the moment with him. They were on the verge of breaking up until they learned their Types, and were able to see they weren't just trying to drive each other crazy, but that there was a reason for their difference.

"Anna"

Here's a story about a Perceiving Type that I have worked with for many years. She is an INFP, extremely sensitive, incredibly loving, very tuned into energy and hates being a P. She gets so mad at herself for being a "go with the flow" person when she is surrounded by J energy. I have been encouraging her to find her tribe so that she feels at home and can start to embrace her awesome INFP self. She had been networking her business with driven, entrepreneurial women and feeling terrible about herself. She finally found a group of Reiki practitioners that share her "go with the flow energy" and also manage successful practices. She is finally starting to see that if she was a J, like she had wished for so many years, she may not be able to do the energy work she does—which takes a soft, "go with the flow" energy of a P.

Which one are you?
Judging or Perceiving?

I have given you as much detail as I can to hopefully give you confidence to choose which one you have a preference for and to what degree (1—30). So, take a moment and choose which one best describes you. Where do you think you fit on the Judging and Perceiving scale? Are you strongly Judging? Are you strongly Perceiving? Or are you somewhere in between? Draw yourself where you think you are the scale.

J 30----------------------------1/1-------------------------30 P

Chapter 6

Marginalized Types

Before we end this section, it is important to remind you of the Types that often feel marginalized. They often describe feeling like they are on the outside looking in, or as if they're weird or have felt odd, misunderstood or left out. If you have felt that way, you are likely one of these Types.

Introverts (I) – We live in an Extroverted world, so oftentimes Introverts find themselves trying hard to fit in by being an Extrovert or doing Extroverted activities.

Intuitive (N) – With only 25% of the population as N Types, our world has been designed for Sensing Types. School, standardized tests, nine to five corporate jobs, four weeks of vacation and M–F work schedules are designed to fit Sensors' here-and-now way of being. Intuitive Types have a very hard time fitting into that.

Feeling men (F) – Roughly 25% of men.

Thinking women (T) – Roughly 25% of women.

Perceivers (P) – We live in a world that rewards structure. Ps prefer to live spontaneously, which can often be met with judgment from our world designed on a time schedule.

INTP women - They often feel the most marginalized because we live in an Extroverted, Sensing, Feeling women, and Judging/planned world.

INFP men – They feel similar for the same reasons as the women above.

Are you in any of these categories? Or, do you know anyone who fits in these categories? Stop judging them and start loving them for their differences. It doesn't mean there is something wrong with them, or you, or any of us. We are who we are, let's start embracing our differences instead of letting them tear us apart.

Chapter 7

Whole Letter Type

Before we can move on to the heart of this book, how to Live Your Life from the Front Seat, you must be confident with your preferences that we spent the last section covering.

....

Extroversion / **I**ntroversion
Sensing / **IN**tuition[2]
Thinking /**F**eeling
Judging / **P**erceiving

....

The four dichotomies are extremely important to understand and invaluable in and of themselves. However, we are about to dig much deeper into you: your energy, how people see you, your best self, how you react during stress and the things you need to avoid in your life, relationships and your work.

At this point, there will be a few of you that are still struggling with determining your Type. In my experience, there are always a few people that have a hard time determining their preference between one or more of the pairings. If that is where you are, this section will help you get clear on your

---

[2]*Myers and Briggs already used "I" for Introvert so please notice that they use the letter N for Intuition*

Type. The Type Table below shows the 16 different Myers-Briggs Types. You have a preference for one of them, again, with varying degrees of strength. If you are struggling between whether you have a preference for Introversion or Extroversion, but you are clear about the last three letters, then read the two descriptions of the two different whole Types and one will resonate much more with you. For example, if you are clear on your NFP but not sure about whether you have a preference for Introversion and Extroversion, then read both ENFP and INFP and one will be a much better fit. You will see there is a big difference between an ENFP and an INFP. One letter makes a huge difference throughout the rest of the book, so it is important to be clear about your Type before moving on.

Type Table

ISTJ	ISFJ	INFJ	INTJ
1. Sensing	1. Sensing	1. Intuition	1. Intuition
2. Thinking	2. Feeling	2. Feeling	2. Thinking
3. Feeling	3. Thinking	3. Thinking	3. Feeling
4. Intuition	4. Intuition	4. Sensing	4. Sensing
ISTP	**ISFP**	**INFP**	**INTP**
1. Thinking	1. Feeling	1. Feeling	1. Thinking
2. Sensing	2. Sensing	2. Intuition	2. Intuition
3. Intuition	3. Intuition	3. Sensing	3. Sensing
4. Feeling	4. Thinking	4. Thinking	4. Feeling
ESTP	**ESFP**	**ENFP**	**ENTP**
1. Sensing	1. Sensing	1. Intuition	1. Intuition
2. Thinking	2. Feeling	2. Feeling	2. Thinking
3. Feeling	3. Thinking	3. Thinking	3. Feeling
4. Intuition	4. Intuition	4. Sensing	4. Sensing
ESTJ	**ESFJ**	**ENFJ**	**ENTJ**
1. Thinking	1. Feeling	1. Feeling	1. Thinking
2. Sensing	2. Sensing	2. Intuition	2. Intuition
3. Intuition	3. Intuition	3. Sensing	3. Sensing
4. Feeling	4. Thinking	4. Thinking	4. Feeling

Now that you've successfully completed the first section, take a moment and put together those four dominant initials as this is your dominant Type. Fill in your whole letter Type here: _____.

Introverted Types:

- ISTJ- The Duty Filler
- ISFJ- The Nurturer
- INFJ- The Protector
- INTJ- The Scientist
- ISTP- The Mechanic
- ISFP- The Artist
- INFP- The Idealist
- INTP- The Thinker

Extroverted Types:

- ESTP- The Doer
- ESFP- The Performer
- ENFP- The Inspirer
- ENTP- The Visionary
- ESTJ- The Guardian
- ESFJ- The Caregiver
- ENFJ- The Giver
- ENTJ- The Executive

Due to copyright laws, I cannot provide you the full Myers-Briggs descriptions (which are the best). But, you can find them on my website at www.jessicabutts.com under the My Book tab. I encourage you to go there now and read about your whole full letter Type. You'll discover positive and negative traits about your Type. Have an open mind. You will probably think something like, "This is so me." Most people feel extremely validated at this point because they have the experience of reading about themselves.

The descriptions by Myers-Briggs are written for people with clear to strong preferences (10–30), so if you have a slight preference (1–9), some of what you read might not quite fit. That is OK. If your personality dichotomy is slight rather than severe, try switching the letter that you feel doesn't describe you well and then find your full Type description to see if that Type sounds more like you. If something about a specific Type doesn't quite ring true for you, look at the pairs again and maybe switch out one of the letters to see if that makes more sense to you. For example, if you are an ENFP but only slight on the P, also read ENFJ and see which one resonates with you more.

At this point you may also want to reach out to a practitioner like myself and take your actual MBTI assessment online so you can see how you come out in comparison to this self-assessment we just did. You can reach me at jessica@jessicabutts.com, or you can find another certified Myers-Briggs trainer.

Excellent work so far!!! I know I've said it before, but this is really just the beginning. Now we are about to have some real fun. I have been using Type for over 20 years, and my "Live Your Life from the Front Seat" method (as well as my unique version of archetypes) will help you see yourself and others in your life so much more clearly. It will give you new language to bring into your life, relationships and your work to help you start living an authentic, genuine and kick-ass life.

Chapter 8

Group/Family Type

If you are like most people, you have undoubtedly been typing your friends, family, spouse, kids and coworkers as we have been going on this journey of exploring your Type. Now that you have your whole letter Type and likely have typed a few others in your life, we can talk about group and/or family Type.

I have talked about the marginalized Types and how tough it can be as the one feeling left out. Well, the same goes for groups or families. The best way I can explain this is to show you a couple of examples. The first is a small company of six where I recently did a workshop.

Here are the employees' Types:

ENFP

ENFP

INFP

ESTP

ISFP

<u>ENFJ</u>

Group Type = ENFP

To determine this group's Type, you simply add up the sum of the letters.

4 Extroverts vs. 2 Introverts = Extrovert **(E)**

2 Sensors vs. 4 Intuitive = Intuitive **(N)**

1 Thinker vs. 5 Feelers = Feeler **(F)**

1 Judger vs. 5 Perceivers = Perceiver **(P)**

This group's Type is an **ENFP** because the majority of the employees are Extroverted, Intuitive, Feeling, and Perceiving; therefore the group dynamic is mostly ENFP.

Once the group could see it laid out like this, the light bulbs starting going off. The manager, the ENFJ and the only J in the group, realized why he had been so frustrated with everyone. He felt as if he was the only one who cared about the small company because he was the only one who came to work on time each day, set and followed all the rules, and couldn't understand their laid-back attitudes. The rest of the group explained it wasn't as if they didn't care, they just had a different way of being, a more laid-back approach to life and business.

The other marginalized person in the organization was a woman and the only Thinker in the group. She always felt as if she didn't want to get involved with the "touchy feely" stuff with customers, clients or the other staff. Once she saw why, she felt as if she could finally verbalize it to the group without judgment. There wasn't anything wrong with her; she was just the only Thinking Type in the group.

My second example is a family of four I worked with a few years ago. Their Types are as follows:

Dad – ENTP

Mom – ENTP

Daughter – ISFJ

Son – ESTP

Family Type = ES/NTP

Their family Type is Extroverted, split between Sensing and Intuition, Thinker and Perceiver. As you can imagine, the daughter (ISFJ) felt marginalized, weird and left out a lot of the time in her family based on the family Type dynamic. Once the family learned all their Types and could see their family Type clearly, they realized they needed to allow their daughter to be alone when she needed to be, without judgment. They also realized she needed a little emotional support to fulfill her Feeling Type and they needed to provide more structure for her J'ness.

Understanding group and family Type can lead to so much more awareness and understanding of each other. I hope this is something you will consider doing with every group in your life so you can better understand the dynamic of the group and where you land in it.

Chapter 9

Archetypical View

There are a number of ways to break down Type. You are already familiar with **dichotomies** and **whole letter Type**.

We started with the individual **dichotomies** by Myers-Briggs that tell us so much about ourselves and our relationships.

As you saw, the **whole letter Type** can be a roadmap filled with words and concepts to help us better understand ourselves and tell others how to treat us.

Another fun way to look at Type is by an **archetypal** view, which can help us get unstuck if we're struggling with a couple of letters in our whole letter Type.

David Keirsey developed archetypes that describe specific temperaments based on the work of Myers-Briggs:

- SJ – The Epimethean Temperament

- SP – The Dionysian Temperament

- NF – The Apollonian Temperament

- NT – The Promethean Temperament

I wanted to provide usable, funny, accurate language to use with family, friends and ourselves to understand the four parts of our innateness.

My experience has always been that, what people don't understand, they don't use. Because of this, I've created my own understanding of the temperaments:

NP – Squirrel
NJ – Entrepreneurs
SP - Just Do It
SJ – The Police

I want to make this work accessible and understandable—something you can talk to your kids about, use at the office, with your partner, friends and family. Over the years, I have discovered my own version of archetypes which are the second and last letter of your Type. I believe not only will you find it accurate, but it is also easy to relate to and easy to understand.

I hope each of these different ways of looking at Type gives you a language and/or framework you can use. We each have these archetypes in our lives, and seeing them from this quirky vantage will, I hope, give you a unique perspective into how we all operate and see the world differently. Again, there is not a right or wrong Type. We are all innately born with our Type so understanding ourselves better can deeply enhance our relationships with ourselves and others.

It is part of my unique brilliance to help people understand complex things in an easy to digest way. I hope these archetypes do just that for you!

NP – Intuitive Perceiving Types
ENFP, INFP, ENTP, INTP

Squirrel

Remember in that movie *UP*, when the dog was paying attention to his owner one moment, but as soon as a squirrel came nearby, he completely lost his concentration and focus and was immediately distracted? Yes? Well, NP Types, that's you.

Intuitive Perceiving Types are very easily distracted by bright and shiny objects. They have a lot of ideas (Intuition), but get easily distracted by the next greatest thing and have a tendency to not follow through (Perceiving).

NPs are the gypsies of the world. They may never seem settled and actually prefer it that way. They are constantly on to the next greatest thing or adventure. They want new, rich, and unique experiences.

As I was working on this book, I did some research on the different archetypes. I interviewed people I know and asked them to share words they felt described themselves well.

NPs described themselves as:

- Creative
- Warm
- Easygoing
- Curious
- Loyal
- Adaptable
- Caring
- Insightful

NJ – Intuitive Judging Types
ENFJ, INFJ, INTJ, ENTJ

Entrepreneur

NJs are the entrepreneurs of the world. They have a lot of ideas just like the NPs, but are decisive decision makers, which means they get a lot of stuff done. Unfortunately, NJs don't work very well with change, as they like things systematic, organized and structured. When things get in their way, it causes them to feel flustered and puts them in their Back Seats (which we are going to talk about in the next section). NJs are not great at the details, but can still get things done.

NJs described themselves as:

- Persistent
- Enthusiastic
- Loyal
- Insightful
- Planful
- Curious
- Compassionate
- Encouraging
- Inquisitive

SP – Sensing Perceiving Types
ESFP, ISFP, ESTP, ISTP

Just Do It

The Sensing Perceiving (SP) Types are all about experiencing the world and everything in it. The Sensing (S) Type is about the here and now and taking in information via their five senses, while the Perceiving (P) Type wants to be spontaneous and just go with it. This combination equals a "Just do it" mentality. Whether they're Introverted or Extroverted, they are fun, active, and engaged people. They do this in many ways, through music, art, climbing rocks, jumping off cliffs—it doesn't matter. They just need to be experiencing something.

SPs described themselves as:

- Playful
- Present
- Empathetic
- Go along with others
- Open
- Listener
- Hearing

- Unscripted
- Fly by the seat of their pants
- Whatever works
- Others first
- Unplanned
- Organized but flexible
- Relaxed

SJ – Sensing Judging Types
ESFJ, ISFJ, ESTJ, ISTJ

The Police

Sensing Judging (SJ) Types are the police. They are responsible, value-driven, hard-working, reliable, but sometimes a little rigid. They like structure, schedules and routine. If anyone needs something done, they know they can count on an SJ to do it. Sensing allows them to be practical and in the moment, while Judging keeps them organized and planned.

SJs described themselves as:

- Disciplined
- Organized
- Trustworthy
- Dependable
- Realistic
- Thoughtful
- Orderly
- Careful

- Innovative
- Risk taker
- Multitasker
- Impulsive
- Optimistic
- Leader
- Driven
- Creative

I love dissecting and playing with the work by Myers-Briggs and creating an uncommon way of looking at it. My intention and hope is that you can see yourself in a new light and use these fun ways to put this amazing tool to work in your life, relationships and career.

We are now going to embark on the ultimate creation of my Intuitive brain, and that is how to Live Your Life from the Front Seat.

Chapter 10

Live Your Life from the Front Seat

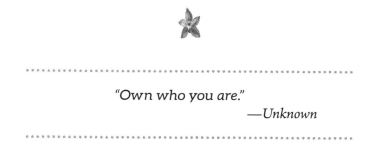

"Own who you are."

—*Unknown*

We have been going over Myers-Briggs work thus far, but I am now going to introduce you to my take on this work, I call it Live Your Life from the Front Seat™. I have noticed a problem over the 20+ years I have been working with Type—people can't remember all the letters; they always struggle with what letters they are, in what order they go and what they even mean. Therefore, they don't use it and that is such a shame because, as I hope you are starting to see, there is great power in understanding your innateness. Living our life based on how we were created is an amazing, congruent feeling and one that I want for all of you!

If you are currently doing a pretty good job of Living Your Life from the Front Seat, then this will further enhance the correct path you are on. But, if you are like most people and living your life from the Back Seat, this section might be a little painful. That is OK, we can change that. There are often tears at this point of my workshop or talk because people realize they have been spending most of their time and energy from the

Back Seat, which you are about to learn is a drain of our energy—big time.

So, now we are going to get even deeper and more specific about your Type and your unique brilliance. The MBTI breaks our Type down into 4 areas that most people find a little difficult to understand.

- Dominant
- Axillary
- Tertiary
- Inferior

I have developed what I hope is a much easier way to understand these four important areas of our personality, how they show up and when. We are going to talk a lot about your passengers for the remainder of this book, and my hope is this will become a new part of your language. I am about to give you a specific roadmap to exactly where you should be spending your energy, your unique brilliance in this world, areas you must avoid and where you go in times of deep stress. You ready? Here we go…

Please imagine a car with four seats. Those four seats represent different parts of your personality; they are all in you, as they are all in the car. You have a Driver and a Copilot, which represent the Front Seats. You have two passengers in the Back Seat that I have named the Drunk Uncle and the Baby in the Back Seat.

- Driver
- Copilot
- Drunk Uncle in the Back Seat
- Baby in the Back Seat

Now, I want you to imagine yourself taking a cross-country road trip. Close your eyes for just a moment after reading this, and really get a mental picture of yourself in your car with you driving, yourself also as the Copilot, an Uncle passed out in the Back Seat and yourself as a Baby in a car seat in the Back Seat. Now, close your eyes and really see this image of these people in your car taking a road trip. This should be an interesting image to see yourself as multiple people in the same car, but this is what your personality Type is like. All these different people are different aspects of your personality.

Now take a moment to take your four letter Type we did in Chapter 7 and correspond it to your car. Please write your words for each passenger (Driver, Copilot, Drunk Uncle and Baby) into the diagram on Page 90.

Use these to find your car description and enter them into the car below. This car can also be found on my website (www.jessicabutts.com) to be printed out to use for yourself or others in your life. I want you to have this visual as we go into the next section. I will outline every car, including yours, but it is important to write this in now so you have it when we cover your Front Seat and Back Seat in detail.

ISTJ-The Duty Filler

Driver: Introverted Sensing

Copilot: Extroverted Thinking

Drunk Uncle in the Back Seat: Introverted Feeling

Baby in the Back Seat: Extroverted Intuition

ISFJ-The Nurturer

Driver: Introverted Sensing

Copilot: Extroverted Feeling

Drunk Uncle in the Back Seat: Introverted Thinking

Baby in the Back Seat: Extroverted Intuition

INFJ-The Protector

Driver: Introverted Intuition

Copilot: Extroverted Feeling

Drunk Uncle in the Back Seat: Introverted Thinking

Baby in the Back Seat: Extroverted Sensing

INTJ-The Scientist

Driver: Introverted Intuition

Copilot: Extroverted Thinking

Drunk Uncle in the Back Seat: Introverted Feeling

Baby in the Back Seat: Extroverted Sensing

ISTP-The Mechanic

Driver: Introverted Thinking

Copilot: Extroverted Sensing

Drunk Uncle in the Back Seat: Introverted Intuition

Baby in the Back Seat: Extroverted Feeling

ISFP-The Artist

Driver: Introverted Feeling

Copilot: Extroverted Sensing

Drunk Uncle in the Back Seat: Introverted Intuition

Baby in the Back Seat: Extroverted Thinking

INFP-The Idealist

Driver: Introverted Feeling

Copilot: Extroverted Intuition

Drunk Uncle in the Back Seat: Introverted Sensing

Baby in the Back Seat: Extroverted Thinking

INTP-The Thinker

Driver: Introverted Thinking

Copilot: Extroverted Intuition

Drunk Uncle in the Back Seat: Introverted Sensing

Baby in the Back Seat: Extroverted Feeling

ESTP-The Doer

Driver: Extroverted Sensing

Copilot: Introverted Thinking

Drunk Uncle in the Back Seat: Extroverted Feeling

Baby in the Back Seat: Introverted Intuition

ESFP-The Performer

Driver: Extroverted Sensing

Copilot: Introverted Feeling

Drunk Uncle in the Back Seat: Extroverted Thinking

Baby in the Back Seat: Introverted Intuition

ENFP-The Inspirer

Driver: Extroverted Intuition

Copilot: Introverted Feeling

Drunk Uncle in the Back Seat: Extroverted Thinking

Baby in the Back Seat: Introverted Sensing

ENTP-The Visionary

Driver: Extroverted Intuition

Copilot: Introverted Thinking

Drunk Uncle in the Back Seat: Extroverted Feeling

Baby in the Back Seat: Introverted Sensing

ESTJ-The Guardian

Driver: Extroverted Thinking

Copilot: Introverted Sensing

Drunk Uncle in the Back Seat: Extroverted Intuition

Baby in the Back Seat: Introverted Feeling

ESFJ-The Caregiver

Driver: Extroverted Feeling

Copilot: Introverted Sensing

Drunk Uncle in the Back Seat: Extroverted Intuition

Baby in the Back Seat: Introverted Thinking

ENFJ-The Giver

Driver: Extroverted Feeling

Copilot: Introverted Intuition

Drunk Uncle in the Back Seat: Extroverted Sensing

Baby in the Back Seat: Introverted Thinking

ENTJ-The Executive

Driver: Extroverted Thinking

Copilot: Introverted Intuition

Drunk Uncle in the Back Seat: Extroverted Sensing

Baby in the Back Seat: Introverted Sensing

Full Car

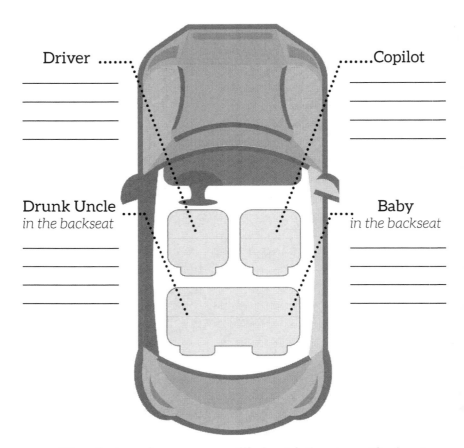

Driver ......

...... Copilot

Drunk Uncle
in the backseat

Baby
in the backseat

Now that you have your car filled out, let's get specific about each of the passengers in your car, and what they represent in your life and your relationships.

Remember the visual of the passengers in your car taking a cross country trip—this is who I am about to describe. If you need further visual help, there are some videos on my website (www.jessicabutts.com) and YouTube channel you can watch to help you get clear!

Chapter 11

Your Front Seat

....

"Beauty begins the moment you decide to be yourself."
— *Coco Chanel*

....

One thing has happened universally to everyone reading this book and everyone on earth—we have all been born. We are all born into this world with our unique and special personality Type for a reason. We are all born with our personality Types and, as I have said before, our Type does not change, our life circumstances change.

So, what happens to pull us away from our innateness is the "crap in our trunks": our family origin, our traumas, that teacher that told us we weren't good enough, traditional schools, college, corporate America and financial responsi-

Can you remember who your were before the world told you who you should be?

bilities. There are so many factors that can keep us from being our Innate self. In the next section, I will address many of them in detail so we can start to explore, address and then put them aside. Then you will gain the power to move through them and start becoming the person you were meant, and innately designed, to be. The fact is, it is easier, and takes less energy, to be who we were designed to be—it just is!

It takes effort to be in our Back Seats and to do things we were not meant to be doing.

There was a philosophy back in the 80s that we should all be balanced and work on the things we aren't good at. I call bullshit on that! Don't do stuff you suck at. Why waste your energy?

We only have so much energy. Why not spend the majority of your energy doing things you are great at? That is where you have your best energy—energy that attracts the right people into your life, makes you more money, and makes you happier. Why would we not do that? Because society tells us differently. Don't listen to them!

Your Front Seat is where you want to be spending at least 80% of your time! I promise you, if you start spending that much time in your Front Seat, your life will change for the better. You will:

- Show up authentically
- Have better energy
- Do better work
- Sleep better
- Have deeper connections with people
- Make more money
- Be happier
- Likely lose weight
- Have better sex
- Feel better
- Feel a sense of freedom
- Attract the right people/clients/friends into your life

Honestly, shame on us for not doing this! If we are wasting our time in our Back Seats (or our trunks) we are doing such a disservice to ourselves, our friends, our jobs, our spouses and our kids! Do you want to be giving your wonky energy to your children? I certainly hope not! So, it is time to start Living Your Life from the Front Seat. I will show you exactly how, now that you know your four letter Myers-Briggs Type. This next section is going to walk you through your Front Seat, your best self, and where you should be spending 80% of your time. And then we will talk about your dreaded Back Seat drivers and where you must stop spending your time. How? By acknowledging you suck at this stuff, and then asking for help in these areas. Ready? Let's go.

#banishshould
—Jessica Butts

Driver:
your best self

Go back to imagining yourself in your car.

Your Driver is in charge of you, it is your best self. When you imagine the car, this is the person who knows where you are going, decides your path, how fast you are going and is steering the car. He/she is actually leading all the others in the car by being in charge. The Driver has their eyes on the road and can see where you are going. This is the person we want to find in you so we can cultivate it and bring it out the most.

When you are living in accordance with your Driver, people respond to you. They are drawn to you. It is your most healthy self, you at your best. It is your unique brilliance in the world. Your Driver (and Copilot, which make up your Front Seat) is you being authentic. And everyone feels better when they are living an authentic life. Everyone.

Now that you have figured out your Myers-Briggs Type, if you're an Extrovert, you're giving your best self to the world. Let me say that again—if you are an Extrovert, you are giving your best self to the world. You are likely very similar in many areas of your life: at home, at work, with friends, with clients. And if you're not, you should be.

If you're an Introvert you're saving your best self for yourself. Most people don't know the best part of you because you save that for yourself or those very close to you. So, what the world sees of you is your Copilot, your second best self.

Copilot:
your second best self

Imagine taking that cross-country trip; your Copilot is an important part of that journey. This part of your personality is your wingman, your Copilot on the journey of life—taking care to change music, get you some snacks, check the Google Map, tell you where to turn and keep you in check. Your Copilot keeps you balanced, and is your second best self.

If you are an Extrovert, your Driver is an Extrovert, which means your Copilot must be an Introvert. If you are an Introvert, your Driver is an Introvert which means your Copilot must be an Extrovert. We can't have our two Front Seat drivers both be Introverted or Extroverted—they must balance each other out. Since this is where we need to be spending 80% of our time, one must be given to the world and one must be saved for ourselves.

If you are an Introvert, you save your best self for yourself and give your Copilot self to the world. If you are an Extrovert, you give your Driver to the world and save your Copilot self for yourself. Same concept, different energy. Neither is better than the other, they are just different.

As an ENFJ, my Driver is an Extroverted Feeler. That means I give my best self to the world. My Copilot is an Introverted Intuitive. That means in my head I'm always generating ideas, always thinking about what's next. We work in harmony because this is my Front Seat. This is where I am my best. I come up with ideas. I have them in my head. I'm thinking about what's next and where I'm going. I'm visioning. I'm future thinking, but I'm also out there in the world giving myself, my *best* self, to the world.

Who are these two people in the Front Seat for you? How do they show up in your life? What do they represent? More importantly, are you using them correctly and to their full potential?

Unfortunately, many of us are not functioning from our Front Seat. We're working in jobs where we are doing things that we're not really that good at and which suck the energy out of us. We're in relationships where we feel we're being drained of energy and life. I know that many people can resonate with this.

Chapter 12

Your Back Seat

"Don't do stuff you suck at."

—*Jessica Butts*

Now onto the two dreaded back seat drivers in your car: the Drunk Uncle and the Baby in the Back Seat. Both show up when you are doing things that you simply should NOT be doing. You know that your Drunk Uncle or Baby is in charge when you feel stressed out and at your wits end. This is not a time you want a drunk person or a baby making any decisions about your life.

Both the Drunk Uncle and the Baby in the Back Seat have bad, wonky energy! You are not at your best when either one of these two Back Seat drivers are in charge! So, let's spend a little time digging into these two very important, but yucky, people in your car.

Drunk Uncle in the Back Seat:
what you should not be doing

Imagine yourself in the car taking that cross-country road trip. The first passenger in the Back Seat is your Drunk Uncle. Unfortunately, we all probably know someone like this in our family, or have been drunk ourselves. Drunks are a mess. They slur their words, they take much longer to do any task or make a decision and likely it won't be done well since it is being done while intoxicated. We are repelled by drunk people—they are annoying and we would rather not be around them. We would much prefer they simply pass out in the back seat and take a little drunken nap.

We all have things in our lives we suck at, and based on your personality, I will show you exactly what they are. I want you to stop doing them, completely, if possible. If you have designed your life around your Back Seat, it may take a while for you to quit doing these completely at first. But as you work through this and I map out your car for you, you will start to see why doing these things does no good for anyone in your life, especially you.

Back Seat energy is a waste of your effort and your time. Imagine a drunk person running your life or your business! No, thank you! Whatever it is, let someone else do it for you. Remember, we can't be good at everything. Give yourself a break and stop trying for goodness sake. Balance is bullshit. Just do what you are good at. You will be happier, make more money and your energy will be so much better!

When we take jobs that suck our happiness or when we stay in relationships that don't make us feel strong, happy and supported, it just makes sense that we feel completely drained of energy.

That is why I want you to start Living Your Life from the Front Seat, not this wonky, drunk Back Seat energy. Ideally, I would like you to spend 0% of your time as your Drunk Uncle, but at the maximum 10 percent.

Baby in the Back Seat:
you under stress

Your last personality Type is your inferior Type, which I call the Baby in the Back Seat. It seems funny, but it's actually quite serious. When you are stressed out, when your back is up against the wall, when someone has pushed you to your limit, when a job has you at our wits' end, your Baby in the Back Seat takes over and your behavior proves it. Whoever your Driver is, your Baby is the exact opposite, and in an extremely negative context.

If your Driver is Introverted, your Baby in the Back Seat is Extroverted. If you're normally quiet and reserved, your Baby comes out screaming and yelling. It scares people because it's behaving the exact opposite of who you normally are. People will say, "Gosh, you're so different," and the reality is—you are. It is so important to not judge yourself about this, but just to be aware of how impactful the Baby in the Back Seat is.

If your Driver is Extroverted, your Baby in Back Seat is Introverted. When you are stressed out or at your wits' end as an Extrovert, you retreat and hide from the world. Your normal outgoing self has to take a break from your normal Extroverted energy, and hides and retreats. Your friends may wonder where you went, why you aren't calling or posting on Facebook—it is likely because you don't want to leave the house or even your bed.

I know I don't want a drunk person or a baby running my life or my business. A drunk is a mess and makes mistakes, and a baby is immature and the opposite of my best self. These two parts of ourselves are extremely dangerous to our energy, our job and our relationships. We need to learn how to keep them to a minimum.

Every time I am giving a talk and I get to the Baby in the Back Seat someone (or multiple people) in the audience begins to cry. That is always a sign that the person has been living their life from the Back Seat and they know how awful it feels to be functioning from this place. Consider these experiences: bad relationships, wrong jobs, doing too much Drunk Uncle activities, someone hurting you. All can keep you functioning in your Back Seat for days or, in many cases, years.

Our reptilian brain and the Baby in the Back Seat

Our brain has many important parts, but the two parts I am going to discuss with you are our prefrontal cortex and our reptilian brain.

Our prefrontal cortex is there for reasoning; it is what sets us apart from all other animals. It allows us to make decisions, have reasoning and be rational.

Our reptilian brain is that of a reptile, its primary function is to fight or flee.

You can think of your Baby in the Back Seat as flipping your prefrontal cortex up and only using/showing your reptilian brain. All our reasoning and rational thoughts have gone out the door. We are solely fighting or fleeing, and we are designed to do one or the other.

Extroverts flee; they run away, they hide. Their typical normal, driver self is out in the world giving their best selves.

Extroverts flee:
they run away,
they hide.

When they are stressed out, at their wits' end or someone hurts them, their prefrontal reasoning goes away and the reptilian brain wakes up to protect them. They do whatever is necessary to retreat.

Introverts fight; they yell, they scream, they pick fights. Their typical normal, driver self is more quiet and reserved,

Introverts fight:
they yell,
they scream,
they pick fights.

saving their best selves for themselves. When they are stressed out, at their wits' end or someone hurts them, their prefrontal reasoning goes away and the reptilian brain wakes up to protect them. They do whatever is necessary to come out fighting.

I want you to take some time to write how your Baby in the Back Seat shows up for you.

_____

_____

_____

_____

_____

_____

_____

_____

_____

_____

Our Baby is going to show up, that is a fact! But, we can also be aware of how and when our Baby shows up and do some things to get us back into the front seat.

Front Seat Activities

Again, it is perfectly okay to get into our Back Seats occasionally. It is going to happen. Instead of beating ourselves up about it, we can sit with it, and then learn some activities to pull ourselves out of that Back Seat and get us back into our kick-ass Front Seat.

Examples of Front Seat Activities:

Extroverts:	Being with people
	Talking with a friend
	Dancing
Introverts:	Cooking alone
	Journaling
	Reading
	Deep conversation with a great friend
Intuitives:	Being creative
	White space to just imagine
Sensors:	Making a list
	Doing something with their hands or body
NP:	Starting a new, fun project
SP:	Being active with hands or body
NJ:	Creating something new
SJ:	Taking care of something

All Types: Taking a walk in nature, either alone or with a friend
Nature and water, it helps ground us.
Make a Front Seat Music playlist
Reaching out for help, every Type needs to know they are not alone.

What are your Front Seat Activities? Make an exhaustive list here. This is incredibly important and we will use this again in the next section.

_____

_____

_____

_____

_____

_____

_____

_____

_____

_____

_____

_____

_____

_____

_____

_____

_____

_____

_____

_____

_____

_____

I rarely do anything in my Back Seat. I have created a life for myself where I don't do any of my Drunk Uncle activities anymore (which, for me, are Sensing activities). I spend less time in my Back Seat than I used to now that I have designed a life for my Type. But, on the rare occasion when I am my Baby in the Back Seat, I don't do anything of importance. I rest and allow the feelings to be with me for as long as they need to. I process fully through journaling, walking, resting, napping or talking to a friend. Then I pull myself out of the Back Seat and get back into my Driver's seat by doing some Front Seat activities.

Here are examples of my (ENFJ) Front Seat Activities:

- Take a walk in nature, being mindful while doing it
- Connect with a friend in person
- See clients
- Do good work
- Type someone
- Listen to fun, upbeat music
- Create something new
- Dance
- Get out of the house

Again, what are yours?

Chapter 13

Introverts:
Your car

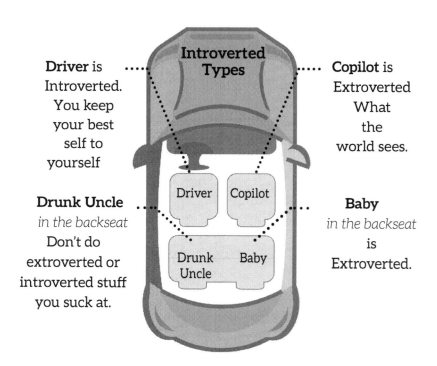

Driver is
Introverted.
You keep
your best
self to
yourself

Introverted Types

Copilot is
Extroverted
What
the
world sees.

Driver | Copilot

Drunk Uncle
in the backseat
Don't do
extroverted or
introverted stuff
you suck at.

Drunk Uncle | Baby

Baby
in the backseat
is
Extroverted.

I want there to be no confusion about how you need to be spending your time, where your best energy comes from, how people are going to be attracted to you, and how you are going to Accomplish Magnificent Things. I have outlined every car so you can clearly see your Front Seat awesomeness and your wonky Back Seat yuckiness.

ISTJ – The Duty Filler

Driver:
Your best self

INTROVERTED SENSING
IN THE INTERNAL WORLD/IN YOUR HEAD:

- You have an internal library of detailed personal knowledge, facts, feelings, sensations and information gleaned from experiences
- Your mind is like a vast internal storehouse of data, details and impressions (internal file cabinet)
- You enjoy rituals and traditions like holidays and birthdays
- You feel comfortable and happy with a day-to-day routine
- You're big on details and data

Copilot:
What the world sees of you, your second-best self

EXTROVERTED THINKING
IN THE EXTERNAL WORLD:

- Order is important to you
- You enjoy organizing both people and things to achieve a purpose
- You use logic and reasoning with others
- You direct action and make decisions
- You are an impersonal decision maker
- You collect information in an orderly way
- You solve problems in a systematic manner

Drunk Uncle in the Back Seat:
Things you suck at and should NOT be doing

**INTROVERTED FEELING IN THE INTERNAL
WORLD/IN YOUR HEAD OR HEART:**

- Dealing with other people's feelings
- Having to explain/explore your values, beliefs and sense of self
- Having to deal with or be sensitive to other people's emotions and inner sensations
- Working in a capacity that requires you to be conciliatory or to create harmony with others
- Doing work which requires you to work with deep internal feelings (yours or anyone else's)
- You need to have people in your life to help you see others' feelings since this is an area you are going to struggle with

Baby in the Back Seat:
Where you go under deep stress or when someone has hurt you

**EXTROVERTED INTUITION
IN THE EXTERNAL WORLD YOU GET LOUD:**

- You express your worries out loud
- Every little thing becomes a huge deal
- If you have a fight with your spouse, you think you are getting a divorce
- You tell everyone what you imagine is going to happen next; the worse your expectation, the more you talk and the louder you get

ISFJ – The Nurturer

Driver:
Your best self

INTROVERTED SENSING
IN THE INTERNAL WORLD/IN YOUR HEAD OR HEART:

- You have an internal library of detailed personal knowledge, facts, feelings, sensations and information gleaned from experiences

- Your mind is like a vast internal storehouse of data, details and impressions (internal file cabinet)

- You enjoy rituals and traditions like holidays and birthdays

- You feel comfortable and happy with a day-to-day routine

- You're big on details and data

Copilot:
What the world sees of you, your second-best self

EXTROVERTED FEELING
IN THE EXTERNAL WORLD:

- You reach out to attach and interact with other living things

- You nurture relationships and connections

- You validate and value others

- You're often found encouraging, coaching, educating and motivating others

- You're good at protecting, helping and caretaking

- You promote collaboration

- You seek harmony in interpersonal relationships

Drunk Uncle in the Back Seat:

Things you suck at and should NOT be doing

**INTROVERTED THINKING
IN THE INTERNAL WORLD/IN YOUR HEAD:**

- Work that requires you to use strict logic and order
- Anything that doesn't recognize your intuitive wisdom
- Activities which require you to internally process and discriminate logic from illogic
- Work that requires you to seek clues and root causes, like a detective
- Having to solve other people's problems (often or repeatedly)
- You need to have people in your life to help you see the logic in situations since this is an area you are going to struggle with

Baby in the Back Seat:

Where you go under deep stress or when someone has hurt you

**EXTROVERTED INTUITION
IN THE EXTERNAL WORLD YOU GET LOUD:**

- You express your worries out loud
- Every little thing becomes a huge deal
- If you have a fight with your spouse, you think you are getting a divorce
- You tell everyone what you imagine is going to happen next; the worse your expectation, the more you talk and the louder you get

INFJ – The Protector

Driver:
Your best self

**INTROVERTED INTUITION
IN THE INTERNAL WORLD/IN YOUR HEART:**

- You see patterns, relationships, symbols, meanings
- You make magical connections to practical problems
- You create a unique vision and arrive at unique insights about things or people
- You can fill in the missing pieces of a life puzzle
- You have complex visions or perspectives that you are unable to explain with clarity to others
- You often ask yourself (and others) "What if…"
- You're always thinking about what's next or how you could be improving yourself or your situation

Copilot:
What the world sees of you, your second-best self

**EXTROVERTED FEELING
IN THE EXTERNAL WORLD:**

- You reach out to attach and interact with other living things
- You nurture relationships and connections
- You validate and value others
- You're often found encouraging, coaching, educating, and motivating others
- You're good at protecting, helping and caretaking
- You promote collaboration
- You seek harmony in interpersonal relationships

Drunk Uncle in the Back Seat:
Things you suck at and should NOT be doing

**INTROVERTED THINKING
IN THE INTERNAL WORLD/IN YOUR HEAD OR HEART:**

- Work that requires you to use strict logic and order
- Anything that doesn't recognize your intuitive wisdom
- Activities which require you to internally process and discriminate logic from illogic
- Work that requires you to seek clues and root causes, like a detective
- Having to solve other people's problems (often or repeatedly)
- You need to have people in your life to help you see the logic in situations since this is an area you are going to struggle with

Baby in the Back Seat:
Where you go under deep stress or when someone has hurt you

**EXTROVERTED SENSING
IN THE EXTERNAL WORLD:**

- You get loud and start bossing people around
- You start obsessing about details, facts
- You demand that people do things a very specific way
- You develop a "my way or the highway" mentality
- You might go into a list making binge
- You want to talk about every detail of a conversation or the way a situation went (especially if it ended badly for you)
- You may go on an eating, drinking or exercise binge

INTJ – The Scientist

Driver:
Your best self

INTROVERTED INTUITION
IN THE INTERNAL WORLD/IN YOUR HEAD:

- You see patterns, relationships, symbols, meanings

- You make magical connections to practical problems

- You create a unique vision and arrive at unique insights about things or people

- You can fill in the missing pieces of a life puzzle

- You have complex visions or perspectives that you are unable to explain with clarity to others

- You're always asking yourself (and others) "What if..."

- You always think about what's next or how you could be improving yourself or your situation

· ·

Copilot:
What the world sees of you, your second-best self

EXTROVERTED THINKING
IN THE EXTERNAL WORLD:

- Order is important to you

- Order the outside world

- You enjoy organizing both people and things to achieve a purpose

- You use logic and reasoning with others

- You direct action and make decisions

- You are an impersonal decision maker

- You collect information in an orderly way

- You solve problems in a systematic manner

Drunk Uncle in the Back Seat:
Things you suck at and should NOT be doing

**INTROVERTED FEELING
IN THE INTERNAL WORLD/IN YOUR HEAD OR HEART:**

- Dealing with other people's feelings
- Having to explain/explore your values, beliefs and sense of self
- Having to deal with or be sensitive to other people's emotions and inner sensations
- Working in a capacity that requires you to be conciliatory or to create harmony with others
- Doing work which requires you to work with deep internal feelings (yours or anyone else's)
- You need to have people in your life to help you see others' feelings since this is an area you are going to struggle with

Baby in the Back Seat:
Where you go under deep stress or when someone has hurt you

**EXTROVERTED SENSING
IN THE EXTERNAL WORLD:**

- You get loud and start bossing people around
- You start obsessing about details, facts
- You demand that people do things a very specific way
- You develop a "my way or the highway" mentality
- You might go into a list making binge
- You want to talk about every detail of a conversation or the way a situation went (especially if it ended badly for you)
- You may go on an eating, drinking or exercise binge

ISTP – The Mechanic

Driver:
Your best self

INTRODUCTED THINKING
IN THE INTERNAL WORLD/IN YOUR HEAD OR HEART:

- Logical order is what is most important to you

- You will dismiss illogic; you will ignore the trivial

- As you take in information, it is logically organized in your mind

- You sort out and discriminate that which makes logical sense from that which does not

- You are like a detective

- You are a problem solver, seeking clues and root causes

Copilot:
What the world sees of you, your second-best self

EXTROVERTED SENSING
IN THE EXTERNAL WORLD:

- You are good at seizing the moment and becoming immersed in the here and now

- You are pleasurably and spontaneously interacting with people, things and situations of interest

- You are good at turning "work" into play

- You enjoy learning by doing (touch it, taste it, hear it, smell it, see it)

- You enjoy new sensory experiences

- You're big on details and data

- You enjoy play

Drunk Uncle in the Back Seat:

Things you suck at and should NOT be doing

**INTROVERTED INTUITION
IN THE INTERNAL WORLD/IN YOUR HEAD:**

- Doing things which require you to see patterns, relationships, symbols, meanings
- Trying to make magical connections to practical problems
- When people expect you to just "understand" them when they don't make sense
- Anything that requires you to fill in the missing pieces of a puzzle
- Activities where you have to think or imagine "what's next"
- Activities which routinely ask you to imagine possibilities
- You dislike all new-age, flakey, woo-woo stuff
- You need to have people in your life to help you see possibilities and the big picture since this is an area you are going to struggle with

- -

Baby in the Back Seat:

Where you go under deep stress or when someone has hurt you

**EXTROVERTED FEELING
IN THE EXTERNAL WORLD:**

- Your normal logical self goes away
- You become intensely emotional
- You may cry, scream, yell
- Your outbursts may cause you to be "in people's faces"— this can scare them

ISFP – The Artist

Driver:
Your best self

INTROVERTED FEELING
IN THE INTERNAL WORLD/IN YOUR HEAD OR HEART:

- You are incredibly sensitive
- You are aware of and cherish your own values, beliefs and sense of self
- You are open to emotions and inner sensations
- You are sensitive to others in an empathetic way
- Authenticity is important to you
- You seek harmony with others and harmony within
- You have deep internal feelings

Copilot:
What the world sees of you, your second-best self

EXTROVERTED SENSING
IN THE EXTERNAL WORLD:

- You are good at seizing the moment and becoming immersed in the here and now
- You are pleasurably and spontaneously interacting with people, things and situations of interest
- You are good at turning "work" into play
- You enjoy learning by doing (touch it, taste it, hear it, smell it, see it)
- You enjoy new sensory experiences
- You're big on details and data
- You enjoy play

Drunk Uncle in the Back Seat:
Things you suck at and should NOT be doing

**INTROVERTED INTUITION
IN THE INTERNAL WORLD/IN YOUR HEAD OR HEART:**

- Doing things which require you to see patterns, relationships, symbols, meanings
- Trying to make magical connections to practical problems
- When people expect you to just "understand" them when they don't make sense
- Anything that requires you to fill in the missing pieces of a puzzle
- Activities where you have to think or imagine "what's next"
- Activities which routinely ask you to imagine possibilities
- You need to have people in your life to help you see possibilities and the big picture since this is an area you are going to struggle with

Baby in the Back Seat:
Where you go under deep stress or when someone has hurt you

**EXTROVERTED THINKING
IN THE EXTERNAL WORLD:**

- You shout, and get in people's faces
- You become loud and bossy in the outside world
- You try to apply a systematic manner to solve problems
- You get out of your heart center and into your head
- You become all cold and impersonal when dealing with people and making decisions
- Your friends will wonder if you got replaced by Spock
- You base everything on reason and logic

INFP – The Idealist

Driver:
Your best self

**INTROVERTED FEELING
IN THE INTERNAL WORLD/IN YOUR HEART:**

- You are incredibly sensitive
- You are aware of and cherish your own values, beliefs and sense of self
- You are open to emotions and inner sensations
- You are sensitive to others in an empathetic way
- Authenticity is important to you
- You seek harmony with others and harmony within
- You have deep internal feelings

Copilot:
What the world sees of you, your second-best self

**EXTROVERTED INTUITION
IN THE EXTERNAL WORLD:**

- You explore new ideas, new people and possibilities
- You are imaginative, inventive and innovative
- You see the big picture and future possibilities
- You naturally energize people
- You engage action towards a vision of what could be
- You're always asking yourself "What if…"
- You are creative
- You often think outside the box
- 75% of people can't see what you see; you have a gift that others need

Drunk Uncle in the Back Seat:

Things you suck at and should NOT be doing

INTRODUCTED SENSING
IN THE INTERNAL WORLD/IN YOUR HEAD OR HEART:

- Anything that requires you to be a virtual repository of data, details and impressions
- Having to remember people's birthdays, anniversaries or other important milestones
- Work that requires you to remember people and/or places and manage minute details and data on a regular basis
- A job that is the same thing, day in, day out—routine kills you
- You need to have people in your life to help you see the facts and details since this is an area you are going to struggle with

Baby in the Back Seat:

Where you go under deep stress or when someone has hurt you

EXTROVERTED THINKING
IN THE EXTERNAL WORLD:

- You shout, and get in people's faces
- You become loud and bossy in the outside world
- You try to apply a systematic manner to solve problems
- You get out of your heart center and into your head
- You become all cold and impersonal when dealing with people and making decisions
- Your friends will wonder if you got replaced by Spock
- You base everything on reason and logic

INTP – The Thinker

Driver:
Your best self

INTROVERTED THINKING
IN THE INTERNAL WORLD/IN YOUR HEAD OR HEART:

- Logical order is what is most important to you
- You will dismiss illogic; you will ignore the trivial
- As you take in information, it is logically organized in your mind
- You sort out and discriminate that which makes logical sense from that which does not
- You are like a detective
- You are a problem solver seeking clues and root causes

Copilot:
What the world sees of you, your second-best self

EXTROVERTED INTUITION
IN THE EXTERNAL WORLD:

- You explore new ideas, new people and possibilities
- You are imaginative, inventive and innovative
- You see the big picture and future possibilities
- You naturally energize people
- You engage action towards a vision of what could be
- You're always asking yourself "What if…"
- You are creative
- You often think outside the box
- 75% of people can't see what you see; you have a gift that others need

Drunk Uncle in the Back Seat:

Things you suck at and should NOT be doing

**INTROVERTED SENSING
IN THE INTERNAL WORLD/IN YOUR HEAD OR HEART:**

- Anything that requires you to be a virtual repository of data, details, and impressions
- Having to remember people's birthdays, anniversaries or other important milestones
- Work that requires you to remember people and/or places, with minute details and data on a regular basis
- A job that is the same thing, day in, day out—routine kills you
- You need to have people in your life to help you see the facts and details since this is an area you are going to struggle with

Baby in the Back Seat:

Where you go under deep stress or when someone has hurt you

**EXTROVERTED FEELING
IN THE EXTERNAL WORLD:**

- Your normal logical self goes away
- You become overly emotional, perhaps even hysterical
- You may cry, scream, yell
- You become confrontational when people upset you; "in their face"

You can tell when people are truly happy.
Their energy is genuine.

—Alex Elle

Extroverts:
Your car

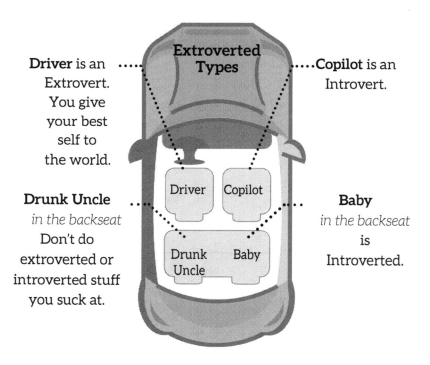

Driver is an Extrovert. You give your best self to the world.

Copilot is an Introvert.

Drunk Uncle
in the backseat
Don't do extroverted or introverted stuff you suck at.

Baby
in the backseat
is Introverted.

Extroverted Types

Driver   Copilot

Drunk Uncle   Baby

ESTP – The Doer

Driver:
Your best self

**EXTROVERTED SENSING
IN THE EXTERNAL WORLD:**

- You seize the moment, and become immersed in the here and now
- You pleasurably and spontaneously interact with people, things and situations of interest
- You're good at turning "work" into play
- You enjoy learning by doing (touch it, taste it, hear it, smell it, see it)
- You enjoy sensory experiences
- Details and data are the way that you take in information and process it
- You are playful

Copilot:
What the world sees of you, your second-best self

**INTROVERTED THINKING
IN THE INTERNAL WORLD/IN YOUR HEAD:**

- Logical order rules all
- Illogic is dismissed as trivial
- Information is taken in and logically organized in your mind
- You sort out and discriminate that which makes logical sense from that which does not
- Like a detective
- Problem solver, seeking clues and root causes

Drunk Uncle in the Back Seat:

Things you suck at and should NOT be doing

**EXTROVERTED FEELING
IN THE EXTERNAL WORLD:**

- Forcing yourself to reach out to attach and interact with other living things
- Trying to nurture relationships, connections or promote collaboration
- Being involved in activities which require you to validate and value others
- Activities where you must encourage, coach, educate or motivate
- Things that require you to act in a protecting, helping and caretaking capacity
- Being in situations that require you to seek harmony in interpersonal relationships
- You need to have people in your life to help you see others' feelings since this is an area you are going to struggle with

Baby in the Back Seat:

Where you go under deep stress or when someone has hurt you

**INTROVERTED INTUITION
IN THE INTERNAL WORLD YOU GET QUIET:**

- You hide in your home, away from friends and family
- You isolate yourself
- Internally you worry
- Every little thing becomes a huge deal
- If you have a fight with your spouse, you think you are getting a divorce
- You start imagining every possible bad thing that can happen to you or your situation

ESFP – The Performer

Driver:
Your best self

EXTROVERTED SENSING
IN THE EXTERNAL WORLD:

- You are good at seizing the moment and becoming immersed in the here and now
- You pleasurably and spontaneously interact with people, things and situations of interest
- You're good at turning "work" into play
- You enjoy learning by doing (touch it, taste it, hear it, smell it, see it)
- You enjoy sensory experiences
- Details and data are your foundation for your experience and knowledge
- You are playful

Copilot:
What the world sees of you, your second-best self

**INTROVERTED FEELING
IN THE INTERNAL WORLD/IN YOUR HEAD OR HEART:**

- You are really sensitive
- You're aware of and cherish your own values, beliefs and sense of self
- You are open to emotions and inner sensations
- You are sensitive to others in an empathetic way
- Authenticity is important to you
- You seek harmony with others and harmony within
- You have and experience deep internal feelings

Drunk Uncle in the Back Seat:
Things you suck at and should NOT be doing

**EXTROVERTED FEELING
IN THE EXTERNAL WORLD:**

- Things that require you to use logic and reasoning with others
- Activities that require you to organize people and things to achieve a purpose
- Projects where you must make impersonal decisions, direct action and be impersonal
- Things where you must collect information in an orderly way, or solve problems in a systematic manner
- You need to have people in your life to help you see logic and reasoning since this is an area you are going to struggle with

Baby in the Back Seat:
Where you go under deep stress or when someone has hurt you

**INTROVERTED INTUITION
IN THE INTERNAL WORLD YOU GET QUIET:**

- You retreat from the world
- You go inward
- You internalize your worry
- Every little thing becomes a huge deal
- If you have a fight with your spouse, you think you are getting a divorce
- You imagine every possible bad thing that could happen to you or a situation

ENFP – The Inspirer

Driver:
Your best self

EXTROVERTED INTUITION
IN THE EXTERNAL WORLD:

- You explore new ideas, new people and possibilities
- You are imaginative, inventive and innovative
- You naturally energize people
- You engage action towards a vision of what could be
- You see future possibilities, and see the big picture
- You're a what-if'er
- You're creative, and think outside the box
- 75% of people can't see what you see; you have a gift that others need

Copilot:
What the world sees of you, your second-best self

INTROVERTED FEELING
IN THE INTERNAL WORLD/IN YOUR HEART:

- You are very sensitive
- You are aware of and cherish your own values, beliefs and sense of self
- You are open to emotions and inner sensations
- You are sensitive to others in an empathetic way
- Authenticity is important to you
- You seek harmony with others and harmony within
- You have deep internal feelings

Drunk Uncle in the Back Seat:
Things you suck at and should NOT be doing

**EXTROVERTED THINKING
IN THE EXTERNAL WORLD:**

- Things that require you to use logic and reasoning with others
- Activities that require you to organize people and things to achieve a purpose
- Projects where you must make impersonal decisions, direct action and be impersonal
- Things where you must collect information in an orderly way, or solve problems in a systematic manner
- You need to have people in your life to help you see logic and reasoning since this is an area you are going to struggle with

Baby in the Back Seat:
Where you go under deep stress or when someone has hurt you

**INTROVERTED SENSING
IN THE INTERNAL WORLD/IN YOUR HEAD OR HEART:**

- You retreat into your own personal world
- You internally obsess about details, facts
- You might go over every detail of a conversation or the way a situation went in your head
- Your head feels wonky, you feel horrible
- You go on a list making binge
- You might go on a food, drink or exercise binge

ENTP – The Visionary

Driver:
Your best self

**EXTROVERTED INTUITION
IN THE EXTERNAL WORLD:**

- You explore new ideas, new people and possibilities
- You are imaginative, inventive and innovative
- You naturally energize people
- You engage action towards a vision of what could be
- You see future possibilities, and see the big picture
- You're a what-if'er
- You're creative, and think outside the box
- 75% of people can't see what you see; you have a gift that others need

Copilot:
What the world sees of you, your second-best self

INTROVERTED THINKING
IN THE INTERNAL WORLD/IN YOUR HEAD OR HEART:

- In your life, logic and order rules
- You dismiss anything illogical as being trivial
- You take in information and logically organize it in your mind
- You sort out and discriminate that which makes logical sense from that which does not
- You are like a detective
- You problem solve, seeking clues and root causes

Drunk Uncle in the Back Seat:
Things you suck at and should NOT be doing

EXTROVERTED FEELING
IN THE EXTERNAL WORLD:

- Forcing yourself to reach out to attach and interact with other living things
- Trying to nurture relationships, connections or promote collaboration
- Be involved in activities which require you to validate and value others
- Activities where you must encourage, coach, educate or motivate
- Things that require you to act in a protecting, helping and caretaking capacity
- Be in situations that require you to seek harmony in interpersonal relationships
- You need to have people in your life to help you see others' feelings since this is an area you are going to struggle with

Baby in the Back Seat:
Where you go under deep stress or when someone has hurt you

INTROVERTED SENSING
IN THE INTERNAL WORLD/IN YOUR HEAD OR HEART:

- You retreat into your personal world
- You internally obsess about details, facts
- You might go on a list making binge
- You go over every detail of a conversation or the way a situation went in your head
- Horrible, wonky, quiet, in your head energy that people do not like
- You may overeat, over-drink or over-exercise

ESTJ – The Guardian

Driver:
Your best self

**EXTROVERTED THINKING
IN THE EXTERNAL WORLD:**

- You are happy when everything is in order
- You organize both people and things to achieve a purpose
- You use logic and reasoning with others
- You direct action and make impersonal decisions
- You collect information in an orderly way
- You solve problems in a systematic manner

Copilot:
What the world sees of you, your second-best self

**INTROVERTED SENSING
IN THE INTERNAL WORLD/IN YOUR HEAD OR HEART:**

- You have an internal library of detailed personal knowledge, facts, feelings, sensations and information gleaned from experiences
- You have an internal storehouse of data and details (internal file cabinet)
- You enjoy rituals and traditions like holidays and birthdays
- Day-to-day routine makes you happy
- You're a stickler for details and data

Drunk Uncle in the Back Seat:

Things you suck at and should NOT be doing

**EXTROVERTED INTUITION
IN THE EXTERNAL WORLD:**

- Forcing yourself to explore new ideas, new people and possibilities
- Forcing yourself to be more imaginative, inventive and innovative
- Trying to see the big picture
- Spending time trying to energize people
- Seeing what possibilities may exist in the future
- Playing "what if" games with Intuitive Types
- Trying to think outside the box
- You need to have people in your life to help you see possibilities and alternatives since this is an area you are going to struggle with

Baby in the Back Seat:

Where you go under deep stress or when someone has hurt you

**INTROVERTED FEELING
IN THE INTERNAL WORLD/IN YOUR HEAD OR HEART:**

- You retreat from the world
- You may not want to get out of bed
- You feel very emotional and overwhelmed by your emotions
- You feel deeply hurt
- Your emotionally distraught and withdrawn behavior worries people in your life

ESFJ – The Caregiver

Driver:
Your best self

**EXTROVERTED FEELING
IN THE EXTERNAL WORLD:**

- You reach out to attach and interact with other living things
- You nurture relationships and connections
- You validate and value others
- You encourage, coach, educate and motivate
- You protect, help and take care of people and things
- You're all about collaboration
- You seek harmony in interpersonal relationships

Copilot:
What the world sees of you, your second-best self

**INTROVERTED SENSING
IN THE INTERNAL WORLD/IN YOUR HEART:**

- You have an internal library of detailed personal knowledge, facts, feelings, sensations and information gleaned from experiences
- You have a vast internal storehouse of data, details and impressions (internal file cabinet)
- You enjoy rituals and traditions like holidays and birthdays
- You thrive in a day-to-day routine
- You're a stickler for details and data

Drunk Uncle in the Back Seat:
Things you suck at and should NOT be doing

EXTROVERTED INTUITION
IN THE EXTERNAL WORLD:

- Forcing yourself to explore new ideas, new people and possibilities
- Forcing yourself to be more imaginative, inventive and innovative
- Trying to see the big picture
- Spending time trying to energize people
- Seeing what possibilities may exist in the future
- Playing "what if" games with Intuitive Types
- Trying to think outside the box
- You need to have people in your life to help you see possibilities and alternatives since this is an area you are going to struggle with

Baby in the Back Seat:
Where you go under deep stress or when someone has hurt you

INTROVERTED THINKING
IN THE INTERNAL WORLD/IN YOUR HEAD OR HEART:

- You hide from the world
- You might obsessively goes over details, facts and data in your head
- You abandon your normal Extroverted Feeling self and retreat into your thoughts
- You may not want to leave the house or be around people
- You internally process logic and data over and over
- You feel icky and gross, as if you have lost your mojo
- You repel people by being in your head and not your heart

ENFJ – The Giver

Driver:
Your best self

**EXTROVERTED FEELING
IN THE EXTERNAL WORLD:**

- You reach out to attach and interact with other living things
- You nurture relationships and connections
- You validate and value others
- You encourage, coach, educate and motivate
- You protect, help and take care of others
- You promote collaboration
- You seek harmony in interpersonal relationships

Copilot:
What the world sees of you, your second-best self

**INTROVERTED INTUITION
IN THE INTERNAL WORLD/IN YOUR HEAD OR HEART:**

- You see patterns, relationships, symbols, meanings
- You make magical connections to practical problems
- You create a unique vision and arrive at unique insights about things or people
- You can fill in the missing pieces of a life puzzle
- You have complex visions or perspectives that you are unable to explain with clarity to others
- You're always thinking "what if"
- You always think about what's next or how you could be improving yourself or your situation

Drunk Uncle in the Back Seat:
Things you suck at and should NOT be doing

**EXTROVERTED SENSING
IN THE EXTERNAL WORLD:**

- Trying to live in the moment and immersing yourself in the here and now
- Trying to interact spontaneously with people, things and situations of interest
- Trying to turn "work" into play
- Managing details and data
- Trying to learn by doing (touch it, taste it, hear it, smell it, see it)
- Having only sensory experiences
- You need to have people in your life to help you see facts, data and details since this is an area you are going to struggle with

Baby in the Back Seat:
Where you go under deep stress or when someone has hurt you

**INTROVERTED THINKING
IN THE INTERNAL WORLD/IN YOUR HEAD:**

- Hide from the world
- Obsessively go over details, facts and data in your head
- Abandon your normal Extroverted Feeling self and retreat into your own world in your head
- May not want to leave the house
- Doesn't want to be around people
- Process logic data over and over again in your head
- Horrible energy; seems as if you have lost your mojo
- Repel people by being in your head and not your heart

ENTJ – The Executive

Driver:
Your best self

**EXTROVERTED THINKING
IN THE EXTERNAL WORLD:**

- Your focus is order
- You organize both people and things to achieve a purpose
- You use logic and reasoning with others
- You are all about direct action
- You are an impersonal decision maker
- You call plays and make decisions
- You collect information in an orderly way
- You solve problems in a systematic manner

Copilot:
What the world sees of you, your second-best self

**INTROVERTED INTUITION
IN THE INTERNAL WORLD/IN YOUR HEAD OR HEART:**

- You see patterns, relationships, symbols, meanings
- You make magical connections to practical problems
- You create a unique vision, and arrive at unique insights about things or people
- You can fill in the missing pieces of a life puzzle
- You have complex visions or perspectives that you are unable to explain with clarity to others
- You're a what-if'er
- You're always thinking about what's next or how you could be improving yourself or your situation

Drunk Uncle in the Back Seat:

Things you suck at and should NOT be doing

EXTROVERTED SENSING
IN THE EXTERNAL WORLD:

- Trying to live in the moment and immersing yourself in the here and now
- Trying to interact spontaneously with people, things and situations of interest
- Trying to turn "work" into play
- Managing details and data
- Trying to learn by doing (touch it, taste it, hear it, smell it, see it)
- Having only sensory experiences
- You need to have people in your life to help you see facts, data and details since this is an area you are going to struggle with

Baby in the Back Seat:

Where you go under deep stress or when someone has hurt you

INTROVERTED FEELING
IN THE INTERNAL WORLD/IN YOUR HEART:

- You withdraw from the world
- You may not want to get out of bed
- You have deep, hurt feelings
- You feel very emotional or overwhelmed by emotions
- When you behave so emotionally, withdrawn and distraught, it worries the people in your life

Summary of Front Seat Activities

To Accomplish Magnificent Things in your life, you must spend at least 80% of your time in your Front Seat as the driver or copilot. Your best energy and your best self shows up when you're in the Front Seat. *Here's a review of Front Seat experiences:*

Intuitives (N)

Extroverted Intuition
IN THE EXTERNAL WORLD:

- You explore new ideas, new people and possibilities
- You are imaginative, inventive and innovative
- You think and see the big picture
- You naturally energize people
- You engage in action towards a vision of what could be
- Future possibilities
- What-if'ers
- Creative
- Think outside the box
- 75% of people can't see what you see; you have a gift that others need

Introverted Intuition
IN THE INTERNAL WORLD/IN YOUR HEAD OR HEART:

- You see patterns, relationships, symbols, meanings
- You make magical connections to practical problems
- You create a unique vision and arrive at unique insights about things or people
- You can fill in the missing pieces of a life puzzle
- You have complex visions or perspectives that you are unable to explain with clarity to others
- What-if'er
- You always think about what's next or how you could be improving yourself or your situation

Sensors (S)

Extroverted Sensing
IN THE EXTERNAL WORLD:

- You seize the moment and become immersed in the here and now
- You pleasurably and spontaneously interact with people, things, and situations of interest
- You're good at turning "work" into play
- You learning by doing (touch it, taste it, hear it, smell it, see it)
- You enjoy sensory experiences
- You easily manipulate and process details and data
- You like doing things with your hands
- You are playful

Introverted Sensing
IN THE INTERNAL WORLD/IN YOUR HEAD OR HEART:

- You have an internal library of detailed personal knowledge, facts, feelings, sensations and information gleaned from experiences
- You have a vast internal storehouse of data, details, and impressions (internal file cabinet)
- You enjoy rituals and traditions like holidays and birthdays
- You're good at day-to-day routine
- You manage details and data well

Feelers (F)

Extroverted Feeling
IN THE EXTERNAL WORLD:

- You reach out to attach and interact with other living things
- You nurture relationships; you validate and value others
- Connections
- You encourage, coach, educate and motivate
- You protect, help and take care
- You promote collaboration
- You seek harmony in interpersonal relationships

Introverted Feeling
IN THE INTERNAL WORLD/IN YOUR HEAD OR HEART:

- You are the most sensitive
- You are aware of and cherish your own values, beliefs and sense of self
- You are open to emotions and inner sensations
- You are sensitive to others in an empathetic way
- Being authentic is important to you
- You seek harmony with others and harmony within
- You have deep internal feelings

Thinkers (T)

Extroverted Thinking
IN THE EXTERNAL WORLD:

- Your focus is order
- You organize both people and things to achieve a purpose
- You use logic and reasoning with others
- You're the "director" in life
- You're an impersonal decision maker
- You call plays and make decisions
- You collect information in an orderly way
- You solve problems in a systematic manner

Introverted Thinking
IN THE INTERNAL WORLD/IN YOUR HEAD OR HEART:

- Logical order rules all
- You dismiss illogic as trivial
- Information is taken in and logically organized in your mind
- It sorts out and discriminates that which makes logical sense from that which does not
- You are like a detective
- You are a problem solver seeking clues and root causes

Summary of Drunk Uncle
in the Back Seat

To Accomplish Magnificent Things in your life, it is critically important to stop doing the things you suck at, and spend less than 20% of your time in the Back Seat. Based on your Type, if these are part of your back seat, when you do them it is like a drunk person doing them. Whether or not your energy is introverted or extroverted with all other passengers of the car, when it comes to the Drunk Uncle, it doesn't matter, I want you to stop doing these behaviors all together!

Intuitives (N)
Extroverted or Introverted Intuition

You suck at:
- Exploring new ideas, new people and possibilities
- Being imaginative, inventive and innovative
- Seeing the big picture
- Playing with future possibilities
- Thinking outside the box; you would rather do it the way it has already been done before
- Woo-woo talk annoys you
- Seeing patterns, relationships, symbols, meanings
- Filling in the missing pieces of a life puzzle

Sensors (S)
Extroverted or Introverted Sensing

You suck at:
- Details, data, facts!
- Seizing the moment and become immersed in the here and now
- Turning "work" into play
- Living in the moment
- Day-to-day routine
- Giving necessary data to people in your life who need it
- Remembering important dates like holidays and birthdays

Feelers (F)
Extroverted or Introverted Feeling

You suck at:
- Reaching out to attach and interact with other living things
- Nurturing relationships
- Validating others feelings
- Promoting collaboration
- Seeking harmony in interpersonal relationships
- Being sensitive to others and your own feelings
- Empathy in work situations or when making decisions
- Accessing deep internal feelings

Thinkers (T)
Extroverted or Introverted Thinking

You suck at:

- Impersonal logic or reasoning
- Organizing both people and things to achieve a purpose
- Making impersonal decisions
- Solving problems in a systematic manner
- Logically organizing information in your mind
- Sorting out and discriminating that which makes logical sense from that which does not
- Problem solving, seeking clues and seeing root causes

Summary of Babies
in the Back Seat

Inevitably, your Baby in the Back Seat is going to show up. You just have to be aware of when the little one is present. Sometimes, you should even allow your Baby to stick around for a while. But, when it has had its say and the tantrum is over, get back in your Front Seat by doing the activities that will put you there.

Introverted Babies
in the Back Seat

Remember, Introvert Drivers are normally rather quiet, somewhat reserved, docile and have an even temper. But when their Babies wake up, they get loud, in your face, and act out in the ways described below.

Extroverted Intuition
IN THE EXTERNAL WORLD, YOU GET LOUD:

- Externally, you worry
- Every little thing becomes a huge deal
- If you have a fight with your spouse, you think you are getting a divorce
- You imagine every little thing that could go wrong
- Everything is a catastrophe

Extroverted Sensing
IN THE EXTERNAL WORLD:

- You get loud and start bossing people around
- You obsess about details, facts
- You demand that people do things a very specific way
- Your way or the highway thinking and way of dealing with people
- You go into obsessive list making mode
- You will want to talk about every detail of a conversation or the way a situation went
- You might over eat, over drink or over exercise

Extroverted Feeling
IN THE EXTERNAL WORLD, YOU GET LOUD:

- Your normal logical self goes away
- You become overly emotional
- You may cry, scream, yell
- Logic goes away and is replaced with uncontrolled emotion, hysterics
- You get in people's faces and it can scare them

Extroverted Thinking
IN THE EXTERNAL WORLD, YOU GET LOUD:

- You get loud and in people's faces
- You begin bossing people and things around in the outside world
- You become impersonal when dealing with people and making decisions
- You try to solve problems in a systematic manner
- You get out of your heart (your happy place) and into your head
- Your normally loving, caring personality becomes cold and logical

Extroverted babies
in the Back Seat

Remember, extroverts are normally out in the world connecting, being social and sharing themselves. However, when their Babies wake up, they hide from the world and may have the thoughts or behaviors listed below.

Introverted Intuition
IN THE INTERNAL WORLD, YOU GET QUIET:

- You retreat from the world
- You internalize your worry
- You imagine every possible thing that could go wrong
- Every little thing becomes a huge deal
- If you have a fight with your spouse, you think you are getting a divorce

Introverted Sensing
IN THE INTERNAL WORLD, YOU GET QUIET::

- You hide from the world, and retreat into your own personal world
- You internally obsess about details, facts
- You go over every detail of a conversation or the way a situation went in your head
- You obsessively go into list making mode
- You give off horrible, wonky, quiet, in your head energy that people do not like
- You may overeat, over-drink or over-exercise

Introverted Feeling
IN THE INTERNAL WORLD, YOU GET QUIET AND IN YOUR HEART:

- You hide, retreat from the world
- You may not want to get out of bed
- You feel very emotional; you experience deep, hurt feelings
- You feel overwhelmed by emotions
- People worry to see you so emotional, distraught and withdrawn

Introverted Thinking
IN THE INTERNAL WORLD, YOU GET QUIET AND IN YOUR HEAD:

- You hide from the world
- You obsessively go over details, facts and data in your head
- You abandon your normal Extroverted Feeling self and retreat into your own world in your head
- You may not want to leave the house
- You don't want to be around people
- You process logic data over and over again in your head
- You feel like you've lost your mojo, lost your energy and zip for life
- You repel people by being in your head and not your heart

We are coming to the close of the first section, and I want you to check in with yourself. How are you feeling? Validated, excited, amazed? I know I was when I learned about personality Type. I was fresh out of college, in my first corporate job when I discovered this life-changing information.

Over the last 20 years I have taken my experience with Type, my skills and education as a therapist, and my own failed marriage to build the method Live Your Life from the Front Seat. I hope you can take this and use it in your life every single day! I want you to use the language provided by Myers-Briggs and me (Driver, Copilot, Drunk Uncle in the Back Seat and Baby in the Back Seat) to transform your life, your business and your relationships.

Before I close the *Who Are You?* section, I have to talk about our nurtured selves. It is going to be a bit of an abrupt change, but absolutely necessary to learn if you are truly going to Live Your Life from the Front Seat and Accomplish Magnificent Things.

Your Type and your innateness cannot change and should not change. Your nurtured self is about the things that have happened *to* you over time and make up a huge part of who you are.

I mentioned earlier in this section that there are influences that take each one of us away from being our Innate selves—the people we were born into this world to be. We must stop fighting against this! I promise that this alone—ending the fight—will change your life. As a therapist, I see the effects of these nurtured issues every single day. They are profound and must be addressed. The most common way I see these issues present themselves is in forms of codependency, which I will address at the end this section.

Chapter 14

Nurture

"People with a high level of personal mastery are acutely aware of their ignorance, their incompetence and their growth areas. And they are deeply self-confident."
—*Peter Senge - The Fifth Discipline*

One of the things that I noticed over the years as a therapist, coach, Myers-Briggs expert, and as I worked on my own life, is that therapy or coaching alone did not take care of the whole person. We need both.

Thus far we have covered your Innate self—how you were born into this world—and primarily worked on traditional coaching.

We also all need traditional therapy to help us figure out our past traumas, our family or origin and the "why" of why we do things. This section is going to cover that part of our lives, but I am not going to dig deep here. If this resonates with you, I urge you to find a good therapist to help you with some of these issues. I have also included a *Resources* section in the back of this book with other books I have read myself and have recommended many times. I encourage you to check them out as well.

When I realized that my work can combine both elements —counseling and coaching—to truly help my clients, I found they were able to live more fulfilling lives. They learned to know themselves, to identify their past patterns and ways of being and thinking, to change those beliefs that no longer served them and to begin to make the changes. I want the same for you.

There is a huge myth out there—that if we don't talk about our stuff, it will go away.

As I mentioned at the beginning of this section, our nurtured self is the person that has developed in response to the environment in which they lived. This can be affected by many factors, depending on their family of origin (FOO), their culture of origin (COO), traumas they may have experienced, birth order, and even unspoken roles and rules within their family. I call this big package of stuff "the trunks of our cars." Sometimes we never open the trunk of the car and examine how this stuff affects us, which keeps us stuck and not moving forward.

There is a huge myth out there—that if we don't talk about our stuff, it will go away. I am here to tell you the exact opposite is true. We must talk about the stuff in our trunks that happened to us throughout our lives because whether we like it or not, it affects who we are and how we show up in this world. There is a saying in Alcoholics Anonymous, secrets keep you sick, and I have found that to be 100% true. The less we talk about something, the more it binds us, keeps us down, and keeps us sick.

There is another saying, "the truth will set you free." I have also found that to be true. We must accept what has happened to us in our lives and open up our trunk every once in a while to acknowledge that stuff is in there. Each time we open it up and talk about it, it loses its control over us. It is a powerful and true phenomenon.

We so often go on through life with these burdens, and wonder why on earth we're feeling overwhelmed and heavy. We forget to open it up, see what's inside and to ditch the junk that's been cluttering our life and holding us back—or at least to come to terms with what's there.

In this next part, we're going to explore all of these sections in your trunks. We're going to look at all of the different compartments. Hopefully this will help you feel like the trunk isn't so full or unwieldy anymore, because you are meant to be living your life from your Front Seat—not how someone else told you to live your life.

What's in the trunk of your car?

You have all seen that car driving down the street that clearly has sooooo much stuff in the trunk that it can't get up to speed. The crap in the trunk is bogging it down. Sometimes the trunk is so full and heavy the car is no longer able to move. We are just like that! We have so much holding us down that we have a hard time moving forward in our lives. Codependency shows up because of this crap in the trunk of our cars.

While where we come from doesn't define us, it does make up a huge part of who we are, whether we like it or not.

As you work through this, you will start to see patterns in your life and in your relationships.

Who we're "supposed" to be

Within families, we are often forced to be someone we're not. Parents don't usually do this on purpose, they just don't know who they are, so they don't know how to allow you to be you either. We are often not allowed to be who we are, if that is different than our family, because it makes them uncomfortable.

There are many Intuitive Types out there that grew up feeling weird, misunderstood or suppressing these creative urges because our parents didn't know what to do with us. Society tells girls they are supposed to be sweet and sensitive, but what if you are a Thinking woman and that just never felt like you? Or you are a Feeling man and grew up with a Thinking mother, and you two just never quite connected and that left you feeling strange and different? Your family's Type can affect how you felt growing up. If you aren't one of the mainstream Types, it could have left you feeling like there was something wrong with you or like you needed to change to fit in.

As I have shared with you, this happened to me many times throughout my entire life, up until the past couple of years. I always wondered what was wrong with me until I finally realized I grew up in a strong family of Sensors, then married an S. I felt different because I *was* different from everyone I had spent most of my life with. When I started meeting other Intuitive Types through networking with entrepreneurial women, I realized these women were like me! I started to embrace my Intuitiveness and I really started to grow.

These trunk situations, however small, become traumas for us. They are the part of our childhood when we weren't allowed to be who we are. Now, I see this a lot, and some-times these children aren't being allowed to be who they are because certain personality Types dominate in the house-hold, or sometimes because of their religious background. No matter the reason why this occurs, these are considered trau-mas in the psyche and affect how we interact with others.

Most of my clients have experienced this type of person-al suppression in their families, but one client in particular comes to mind; we will call her Connie. Connie grew up in a great household—loving parents, one sister, educated, middle class, what most everyone would wish for in a family of ori-gin. Both her parents and sister were strong **Extroverts**, and Connie, as an introvert, always felt like she wasn't able to keep up with the energy of her outgoing, domineering family. All three were also strong **Sensing** Types and expected Con-nie to get the grades her sister did, although because Connie is/was extremely smart as a strong Intuitive Type, she didn't do well in traditional schooling with standardized tests, so she always felt less than and ended up not going to college because she believed she couldn't keep up. Connie is also the only Feeler in her family of **Thinkers,** which made her feel over—emotional and flakey compared to her logical family. And lastly, Connie is a strong P, a dreamer, a gypsy and her entire family, until today, make her feel like a loser and a flake for choosing her own unique life path. She spent 30+ years living a life for THEM until she finally realized how miserable she was, and since then has decided to change her life to live it for her INFP Type. I tell you Connie's story so you can see that trauma doesn't have to be something like abuse in order for it to affect our entire lives. Our family of origin is often the first source of trauma in our life. So it's important to take the time to write down what traumas you might have experienced in your life. Don't belittle your traumas. They could be anything, from your parent telling you that you're useless, to being left alone while a parent lay passed out drunk on the sofa. It could be that your parent ignored you or diminished your feelings. In the space below, take some time to write down any of the things that you can remember right now that made you feel hurt or sad or that have stuck with you. Trauma is trauma, no matter what the severity, and it sticks with us for a lifetime. Remember, secrets keep you sick and they bog down the trunks of our cars. We are here to unleash the secrets that have been keeping you from living the life you are meant to live. These "stories" we have been told are not true! They are not from bad people, they were just told to us from people who didn't know any better and were likely just scared themselves. Let's release them, and yourself, from these lies that were told to you as a child. They are keeping you sick, small and not allowing you to be free to Live Your Life from the Front Seat.

So, make a list of the times you have been told things that hurt you, kept you small or didn't resonate with you, but hurt you none the less.

_____

_____

_____

_____

_____

_____

_____

_____

_____

_____

_____

_____

_____

_____

_____

_____

_____

While you're doing this, try to also think of other parts of your life that have affected your personal history and can be related to traumas that you experienced. In the space provided, fill in your birth order and how that has affected your sense of self. If you are the first born, what things did your parents expect of you that they didn't expect of your siblings? If you're the baby of the family, what did you get away with that no one else did? If you're a middle child, how did that affect your relationship with your parents or siblings?

Birth Order: _____

_____

_____

_____

_____

_____

_____

_____

Next write down any roles that people took up in your family, as well as any unspoken or implied rules that your family had. Example: good girls don't speak up for themselves, or you must get good grades in math and science to be smart or arts aren't a real life path.

Rules and Roles: _____

_____

_____

_____

_____

_____

_____

_____

_____

_____

_____

_____

_____

_____

_____

_____

I also want you to think about culture of origin, if your culture played into the way that you were raised, as well as any religious aspects that were important for you.

Culture of Origin:

_____

_____

_____

_____

_____

_____

_____

Religion: _____

_____

_____

_____

_____

Lastly, write down any patterns that you can spot, such as alcoholism, depression and infidelity.

Patterns:

_____

_____

_____

_____

_____

_____

_____

Codependency

Many of you are likely in some form of a codependent relationship, and it is critically important to learn how you are playing this game with people in your life so you can stop that unhealthy behavior. As you start to live your authentic life and Live Your Life from the Front Seat, you may experience some pushback from people in your life. I want to show you what codependency looks like so you can start to "stay on your side of the net."

I often say you can't un-know what you know, and I hope this book has been an experience like that for you. I hope you are seeing yourself in a whole new way, and are excited to start Living Your Life from the Front Seat. You now know something new, different and powerful about yourself that you cannot un-know. So, the only thing to do is live your life accordingly now. Sometimes changes need to happen in our relationships in order to make that happen.

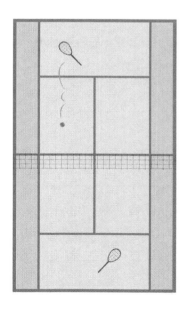

Again, I warn you, this is going to challenge you, your relationships and your belief system, but it can also set you free and make you much, much happier!

I want you to imagine a tennis court, similar to the image at right. There are two people on the tennis court, playing a game together. Each side of the net is each person's own territory, or their side of the net. They are responsible for it—to take care of it, make sure it is healthy, happy, and secure. It is where you are allowed to have your own opinions, beliefs and personality Type. We all need to manage our own side of the net in order to be in healthy relationships.

But what happens in almost all unhealthy or codependent relationships is you'll do one of two things:

- You jump on the other side of the net to manage and control people or things in your life.

- Alternately, you allow other people to come into your court, on your side of the net, to manage and control you. You lose your voice.

When we are not comfortable with ourselves or don't know who we are, we are more likely to try to manage or control others or allow others to control us.

In my experience, Feeling (F) and Perceiving (P) Types have a tendency to be more of the codependent Type that allows others to jump on your side of the net and manage and control you.

Thinking (T) and Judging (J) Types have more of a tendency to be the codependent Type to jump on the other side of the net and manage and control other people.

Both of those situations are codependent behavior, and it is not healthy for you or your partner. This shows that you are not comfortable knowing who you are, standing up for yourself, having a voice and managing your own side of the net.

When we are not comfortable with ourselves or don't know who we are, we are more likely to try to manage or control others or allow others to control us. Now that you know your Type and are hopefully starting to Live Your Life from the Front Seat, you can start the process of becoming healthily detached, and not codependent. You can start to design your own side of the net, find your voice, know what you are great at, become comfortable with who you are and live a life that makes you happy and proud. You will have no need to control others or be controlled when you can do that.

How we choose to respond to something is our choice and can change our lives. Healthy detachment looks like two people in any relationship having their own feelings, ideas and lives while trusting the other person to do the same. There is no need to manage or control the other person because your own life is under control and you trust the other person to have control over their own. Even if you can't trust the other person to do so, you must learn how to get back on your side of the net and only manage and control yourself! You cannot control another person, you can only control yourself.

Viktor Frankl talks about this in his epic book, *Man's Search for Meaning*. There is a space for personal freedom between the stimulus and our response. How we choose to respond to something is our choice and can change our lives. Learning how to be healthily detached instead of being codependent is that personal freedom. It will change your life.

So, first and foremost, you need to tend to your own side of the net before you can expect to be in a healthy relationship with someone else. Unfortunately, if the person that you are in a relationship with is not doing their work, this may be challenging for you both.

This is a huge concept that I am simply introducing you to. If this is resonating with you, I highly encourage you to pick up books by Melody Beattie. When I read her book, *Codependent No More*, many years ago, I was recently separated from my husband and my therapist suggested I might be codependent. While I was a little offended (as most of my clients are when I suggest they might be as well), I was also intrigued and interested in doing anything it took to get healthy.

One Sunday morning, I started reading *Codependent No More*, and I couldn't put it down. At one point, I literally threw the book on the floor as if it was on fire and yelled aloud, alone in my apartment, "Oh my gosh, I HAVE THAT!" It was as if someone was writing about me and how I had been acting most of my life—I just didn't realize it was an actual thing. Well, it is. And learning about it, using it in my life every single day and recovering from it has changed my life in so many ways.

I must warn you, this is not a quick process; it is a lifelong process. I call myself a recovering codependent, as I have frequent relapses of allowing others to manage and control me, or wanting to jump in and fix something when it is none of my business. Having the awareness of who I am, my Type and my form of codependency has brought so much calm into my life and given me so much more energy since I am not worrying about or managing things I don't need to be a part of. It is the most freeing feeling in the world! I want that for you too!

Almost all of us are codependent in one or more ways, because we have simply learned to be that way. However, we are uncomfortable looking at ourselves as being part of the problem. It is easier to blame other people than to look at yourselves, but this book is about looking at yourself, learning who you are and embracing that! You can do this!

Understanding Type and learning about codependency has changed my life and so many of my clients' lives. I encourage you to start accepting who you innately are, living accordingly and then start living a healthy, detached lifestyle.

We are now going to take everything you have learned about yourself in this section of *Who are you?* and apply it to designing a magnificent life for you! Let's explore, *Where are you going?*

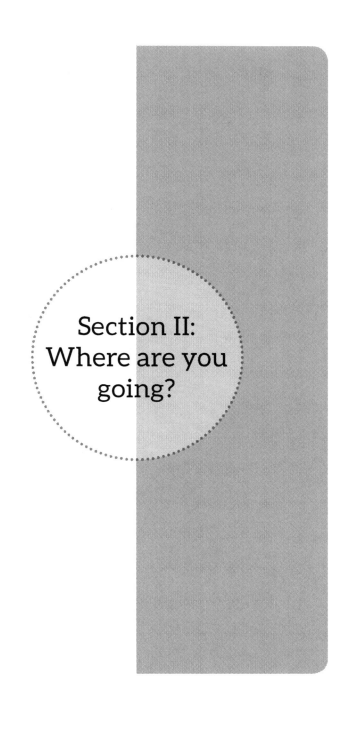

Section II:
Where are you
going?

Chapter 15

Roadmap to Your Life

> "She believed she could, so she did."
> —*Unknown*

As I mentioned in the last section, we need both a therapeutic approach and a coaching approach to our lives to help us make lasting change so we can truly Accomplish Magnificent Things. The entire first section was a mix of understanding your Innate self and your nurtured self.

Now that you know who you are, your Innate gifts, unique abilities, your family of origin and codependent style, it's time to ask:

- What are you going to do with this knowledge?
- Are you going to continue to do what you are doing now?
- Are you content with that?
- How do you incorporate Front Seat activities into your life?

If your response is that you're not happy right now, and you want to change your direction, first you need to ask yourself:

- Where are you going?

- How do you want to design your life around the question of who you are?

In this section, we're going to explore your thoughts and beliefs, and how you can change them to create the life of your dreams with a few simple, yet extremely effective, tools.

The last chapter was all about finding out who you are and what you have been taught to be. Or what you have been told to be. Or what you decided, many years ago, to be, because of what was happening to you then.

By exploring your beliefs now, you are free to choose whether you want to continue to believe those things now. That's right. You are now free to choose whether you want to keep doing what you have done before, whether you want to keep believing the things that have made you play small and not Live Your Life from the Front Seat.

You're here now, so my guess is that you want to make some changes in your life. In order to be able to change your beliefs, you first need to explore what you already believe about yourself and your world. Let's start off with exploring what you currently believe, and move on to how you can change those beliefs to create the life you want.

Over your lifetime, you have come to believe things about yourself and your world that you think are true. Some of these beliefs were taught to you, some you got from observing how your family behaved around these issues.

For example, a child whose parents were always worried about having enough money to pay the rent/mortgage might believe that it's tough to earn money, to support a family and that they never have enough. A child whose parents go through a messy divorce might believe that marriage is a horrible choice and that they're better off being alone.

I've provided a few statements in the space below to get you started. Take the time here to explore some of your own beliefs about these things. If you run out of space, be sure to write the statements of what you believe now into your journal. We'll come back to these beliefs in just a minute.

I believe that marriage is_____
_____

I believe that money is_____
_____

I believe that relationships are _____
_____

I believe that I'm_____
_____

I believe _____
_____

I believe _____
_____

I believe _____
_____

I believe _____
_____

I believe _____
_____

Some of the beliefs you have are **limiting** beliefs. These beliefs are keeping you from Living Your Life from the Front Seat. They are keeping you from being abundant. They are keeping you from being yourself. They are keeping you from having love in your life. They are keeping you from joy and happiness. As you discovered when you explored some of your current beliefs, you probably found that there were a few beliefs that didn't quite mesh with who you want to be.

In the space below, write down some of those beliefs that no longer serve you.

_____

_____

_____

_____

_____

_____

_____

_____

_____

In this next section, we're going to work on ways that you can change your mind and change your beliefs so that you are able to Live Your Life from the Front Seat. Many of them you have likely heard of before, some you haven't. Either way, I want you to come at them with a new attitude and fresh new perspective. These are truly life changing tools, and now that you know yourself much better, it is time to do them from that new vantage point. Got it? OK, let's go.

Mindset

You've probably heard a lot lately about this thing called "mindset" or the "law of attraction." The most basic way I can break it down is this:

....

We are what we think about all day.
What we think about all day, we become.
What we think about expands.

....

That is really all there is to it. If you are thinking about negative things, if you are thinking about where you could be, or where you should (#banishshould) be, or focusing on the thing you are trying to back away from, you are never going to get to where you need to be, ever. You need a mind shift change!

Have you ever wanted to move on from an experience that was negative and end up finding yourself in a similar situation a little later in life? Many people do just that, and they end up repeating history rather than moving on. Why? The reason this happens is they are often looking back, rather than looking forward.

If you want to move forward, you can't be looking back all the time to see where you are in relation to where you came from. If we're going to use the driving metaphor again, it's hard to go forward and get to your destination if you are only looking out your rearview mirror. You're going to crash into something, and chances are it's going to look a lot like the wreck you left behind.

You need to turn away from that past, and focus firmly on what's next. You have to leave that wreck in the rearview mirror behind, and look at the road in front of you. Be aware of your surroundings and what's going on around you so you can navigate confidently to your destination.

What are those wrecks that you're leaving behind you? They're your traumas. Your failed relationships. They're false beliefs about yourself and the way the Universe works. If you continue to focus on your past, you become a victim of your history.

> *"If you don't make the time to work on creating the life you want, you're eventually going to be forced to spend a LOT of time dealing with a life you don't want"*
>
> —*Kevin Ngo*

I'm calling you out, and telling you this backwards thinking has to stop! You can't keep focusing on what you don't want if you want to move forward. You have to turn away from it and focus on something that you truly want. If you continue to focus on what you don't want, you end up attracting the thing you least desire. I believe this is where almost everyone gets stuck.

My mentor calls this behavior "chaotic energy", but I prefer to call it "wonky energy." If you've ever dealt with a two-year -old, you know that they don't understand the word "don't." Your subconscious mind and the Universe are a lot like a two-year-old child. If you say, "I don't want to be broke," your subconscious mind and the Universe don't hear the word "don't," they hear "I want to be broke" and help you get there. Saying, "I don't want to be broke," doesn't make sense to the Universe. The Universe does not know what that energy means. All it hears is "broke." You might say or express "I don't want to be in this bad relationship anymore." But what the Universe hears is "bad relationship."

So your challenge is deciding what you're going to do about that decision to leave that bad relationship behind. What will you focus on? How are you going to focus your energy and attention to a positive place? By turning towards, and focusing on, the life you are designing for yourself.

I recently had a client who kept saying she wanted to be in a relationship, but the more she kept talking, she kept contradicting herself by saying things like, "I am not sure I want to give up my freedom. I really do like being single. I enjoy my alone time, there aren't any good men out there anyway." While that may have also been a defense mechanism, which we explored together, either way she was giving wonky, confusing energy to the Universe.

> *"I know for sure what we dwell on is who we become.*
> —*Oprah Winfrey*

I had a wonky energy experience too. I created a boot camp a few years ago that didn't quite feel right. I worked really hard to make it a success, but deep down I knew it wasn't the work I was supposed to be doing. So, while I asked and asked for the Universe to bring me clients for it, I didn't believe because I couldn't visualize doing that work long-term. It was chaotic energy.

The lesson is this: if you are asking for something and it is not coming, you need to check with yourself to make sure it is what you really want, that your energy is in alignment and that you really believe it. We are co-creators of our experience, and our world, with Universe and God. It is a team effort and we must be in alignment with our team!

For just a moment, try this exercise:

In the room where you are now, imagine the thing that you are trying to move on from in one corner of the room. This can be anything: a bad relationship, a death or anger towards someone. Now step back, but stay focused on it.

Can you see anything else? Probably not. All your attention and focus are on the thing that you don't want in your life.

Slowly turn around and imagine, in the other corner of the room, the things you do want: love, freedom, fun, a career you love, travel, friends or fulfillment—whatever you truly want for yourself. You must shift your mental focus to the new in order for it to come to you. In order to succeed and to reach your goals, you must turn towards the thing that you want to go towards.

Before we move on, I want to give you a couple of examples of things in my life I believed would happen, not just things I hoped would happen.

- I KNEW I would have a successful and full private practice. I knew it, I believed it and therefore I took every action necessary to make that happen. I saw it before it was even a reality.

- I have also visualized places I would live far before I moved there. I imagined the color of the walls, the things that would surround me, where it was in the Seattle area. I have lived a couple of places that I have visualized before I even knew they existed.

I also do this exercise with almost every important day in my life. I create it in my mind before the event actually happens. When I speak, I see the room where I will be speaking. I see the crowd responding to me. I play out in my mind how I do, how I feel, what I say. It is not rehearsed word for word, but rather I see how the entire thing plays out.

In short, our mind doesn't know the difference between

our imagination and reality. You have the power to create the reality that you want rather than what you have always had before!

So how do you do this? And what does it have to do with Type? Well, to start with, as we already know, Intuitive people are natural daydreamers (and dreamers as a whole). They're always imagining "what if", both for good and ill. Sensing Types are more likely to live in the moment and not spend time imagining or dreaming about what they truly want or desire.

But this is where I ask you to both make a commitment to shift your reality, by learning and doing daily visualization exercises. Sensors will typically say "show me" and ask for proof, but I'm going to challenge you to suspend disbelief in this sort of thing, and just trust me that it works, because it most certainly does. It only takes you a few minutes each day to work on your visualizations in order to create the life of your dreams. Plus, it's fun and you will thank me!

The Vortex and the Front Seat

Before you begin the visualization work, it's important for you to first get into your Front Seat as we talked about in the last section. This is the first time we are going to put your Front Seat Activities into use.

Abraham-Hicks coined a phrase about "getting into the Vortex" in their book, *Ask and it is Given*. The Vortex is the equivalent of being in the Front Seat, which is all about being in alignment with your best self and the Universe. When you are in your Front Seat, you are in a place of believing and authenticity. Being in your Front Seat gets you into the Vortex—doing things that make you happy, bringing energy and renewing your soul.

But if you've been living from the Back Seat for a while, it might be tough to get into your physical/emotional/spiritual Front Seat. One of the best ways to do that is to do something that you enjoy. Again, as we discussed earlier, this is time to practice those activities. Here is a short reminder of some activities based on your Type:

Extroverts: Being with people
Talking with a friend
Dancing

Introverts: Cooking alone
Journaling
Reading
Deep conversation with a great friend

Intuitives: Being creative
White space to just imagine

Sensing:	Making a list Doing something with their hands
NP:	Starting a new fun project
SP:	Being active with hands or body
NJ:	Creating something new
SJ:	Taking care of something

> *"Don't be afraid to give yourself everything you've ever wanted in life!"*
> —*Unknown*

The Vortex and being in your Front Seat are all about doing things that make you feel good and get you into your rhythm and best space. For me as an ENFJ, I like to listen to music that gets me in a good mood, dance, allow white space for creativity, check things off my to do list, have a deep conversation with a friend, or take a walk in nature.

What are your Front Seat Activities again? Have you thought of any more? List them here:

_____

_____

_____

_____

_____

_____

_____

Now that you have a list of a few things, do them! The next chapter is going to be all about action, and these are part of your new normal—things you do every day to get you to be your best self. You must, must, MUST do these. Ideally every day, but at least four to five times a week. Notice your energy shift. You will be amazed.

Manifesting practices

OK, are you ready? This is going to stretch some of you. It is going to feel strange to not focus on the things you are trying to move on from, but stick with me. This is all about you and it is based on your Type.

You need to be in your Front Seat to begin this work; you must be in a place of authenticity. You can only look forward when you are in your Front Seat. Let me say that again—you can only look forward and manifest your dreams when you are in your Front Seat. Our Back Seat is looking back. It is scared, fearful, worried and not in alignment with the Universe. Remember, it has the energy of a drunk and a baby, we do not want these parts of ourselves running any part of our lives. So, if you need to get into your Front Seat, please try to do so now by doing a few of the exercises you listed earlier.

Some questions to ask yourself as we go along these exercises:

- What do you want in your life?

- How do you want to feel?

- How do you want to spend your time?

- Who you want to spend your time with?

- What kind of impact do you want to make on the lives of those you love?

- What daily or weekly activities do you want to incorporate into your life?

- What kind of work do you want to be doing?

- How do you want to look?

- What kind of environment do you want to live in?

I use a variety of different mind-shifting activities for myself and to help my clients improve their lives. In this next section, I'm going to go through these different activities and how they might help you make your shift happen.

- Visualization
- Goal cards
- Vision boards
- Books
- Meditation
- Gratitude journal
- Core desired feelings
- Like-minded people

These tools will help keep your car on your new road!

Chapter 16

Visualization

"Change your thoughts and you'll change your world."
—*Unknown*

How do you get clear on what you want? One of the tools I have used throughout my life to help me accomplish what I wanted has been visualization. It is also where you need to start.

Visualization is using the imagination to create a picture of what your desired outcome will be. If you want to be successful, how does that look to you? How is your physical health? How are your relationships? Where is your house? What kinds of vacations are you taking? How often do you work? What kind of work are you doing? When you can create a visual picture in your mind of the life you want to lead, you are already helping the Universe (or God) to help you get where you want to go.

As I mentioned earlier in this section, your brain and subconscious do not know the difference between imagined and real. So, by visualizing, you are tricking yourself into believing it is already happening. You have the feelings associated with already having the thing you want in your life. For example, if you want a wonderful, loving relationship, imagine having it every day, feel what it feels like to have that relationship, imagine you together with your partner, the things you do together, how you look at each other, where you go, how you have sex, how you make each other feel. Imagine it all as if it is happening!

Some people might call it daydreaming, but it's really simply creating that picture, that feeling, of what you're going to do. I did this a lot when I played softball in high school. I would imagine myself running and catching the ball and throwing it and making a great play. I would do it over and over in my head, and I know that it helped me be a stronger ball player.

As I mentioned earlier, I do this when I speak as well. I do this when I have to have a difficult conversation or do anything that I really want in order to trick my mind and subconscious into believing it has already happened the way I want it to happen. And it seriously works!

The crazy part about all of this is that you have control over your own life because you have control over your own thoughts! For some of you that is good news and for some that is a very scary thought. Either way, it is 100% true. So, what do you want to do—create a crappy life or create an awesome one?

Even pro athletes do this. Recently, I read that the world champion Seahawks quarterback, Russell Wilson, does the same sort of thing. Before the game, Russell goes down onto the field and visualizes his game for the day. He sees the play, the ball, how he throws, everything. Olympic athletes do this. Skaters, skiers, swimmers, wrestlers, lifters, runners—they all do it. They visualize their performance first and then they do it.

As I mentioned before, back when I was working in corporate America over ten years ago, I knew that I was going to have an office with my own private practice. That was despite all the naysayers who told me that I was crazy to dream this dream. My ex-husband told me I was crazy. My colleagues in corporate America told me I was nuts. But every night, before I drove home, I could see that there were therapists' offices in my office building. I said "That's where my office is going to be." When I graduated, I went back to that building and lo and behold, there was an office for rent. I walked in and told the management, "I don't even care how much this costs, this is where I am supposed to be. I'll take it." People in the industry (psychotherapy) told me that there was no way I was going to be able to build my practice to a profitable place within three years, but I knew I could. I had seen it already happen in my mind. I achieved my goal in less than half that time; in just a year and a half I had a full practice.

Now, those same people who were my naysayers are coming to me and asking me how I did it. How I got the office I wanted, where I wanted, with the work that I wanted to do. It all comes down to my mindset. I just knew it. I visualized it, I saw it and I believed it. I also worked my butt off, as simply visualizing, seeing and believing isn't enough. I had to put my belief into action (which is the final part of this book).

I also have a not so positive example, but one that is just as powerful, and I hope it helps you think about the positive and negative mindset beliefs you may already have. I didn't realize it when I got married that I had a belief that it wouldn't last forever. That was not a conscious thought, but a subconscious belief based on my family, as they were all divorced. This was pointed out to me years later in therapy with my ex-husband. It was a huge wake-up call for me about the power of our subconscious beliefs.

All of these tools are amazing, but being able to visualize is at the core of all of them. Again, this technique is going to be easier for Intuitive Types because our brains are already designed to do this, but Sensors can certainly do this as well.

Judgers will likely want to do all of these right away. If you can do that, great, but you may also want to do one or two immediately and add the rest in later. The Perceivers are likely to be excited about trying them all, but may not follow through on any of them. So, I encourage you to do these with a friend, and hold yourself accountable to start incorporating these techniques into your daily life.

> *"If you can dream it, you can do it"*
> —*Walt Disney*

So, what do you need to do? It is quite simple really. We will talk more about it in the meditation section, but you simply close your eyes and see it already happening. It can take one minute or two hours or longer. Start to visualize the things you really want in your life with the following exercises I am about to teach you.

Chapter 17

Goal Cards

*"Maybe you have to let go of who you were
to become who you will be."*

—*Carrie Bradshaw*

As an Intuitive Type, I am an intensely visual person. I have always been able to create my own pictures in my head, to visualize the things that I wanted. Because of this, it has always just come naturally to me to do visualization, and see myself doing what I wanted to be doing. But when I learned about and started using goal cards in September of 2013, my successes exploded exponentially!

The SMART goal-setting system attributed to Peter Drucker is a great tool for Sensing Types to use. But you Intuitive Types may have felt constrained or restricted using this tool—I know I did. Peter uses SMART to represent goals that are Specific, Measureable, Achievable (although I say dream big), Relevant, and Time-bound. Sensing Types love these metrics. Intuitive Types need a little more wiggle room, but something just as powerful. Whatever your Type, Sensing or Intuitive, you must try goal cards.

So what is a goal card? It is a card or anything else you choose to write on. What do you want? Write a description of what you want as if your goals have been achieved.

Then, read your goal cards every single day. This daily practice powerfully reinforces your visualizations.

Here's an example that an aspiring marathon runner might use:

"I am at the Boston Marathon. I feel full of energy, my body is healthy and strong, my mind is clear and I am running my best time ever, placing me in the top twenty."

Another example of a goal card could read:

"I am working in the career of my dreams. I easily and effortlessly find the perfect new job. I am happy, fulfilled and making great money. I come home to my family at the end of the day full of love and energy."

A goal card can contain anything you want. It can be a sticky note. It can be a file card. The key to making a goal card is that you write down exactly what you want and then look at the card every day, and read the card aloud often. It doesn't have to be all fancy, but if you're like me, a bit of sparkle and prettying up helps me to have even better thoughts and feelings about those goals that I have expressed. So if flowers make you feel happy, feel free to decorate your goal cards with flowers. If sparkle makes you feel happy, decorate it with sparkly things. If cars or planes or exotic locations make you feel happy, use those too. You can make it as simple or as loud as you want—it's your goal! Once it is written, you need to read it aloud as often as possible. My friend, Kris, taught me that reading things aloud is better than reading them to yourself (although that is also helpful), because our throat is our manifestation center. So it helps to read it aloud in order to believe it.

You can use any 3x5" note-cards but why not have pretty ones like these? You can purchase them at my website.

(www.jessicabutts.com).

You can leave your card anywhere in your house, car or office, as long as it's someplace where you're going to see it and read it often. I display mine next to my nightstand. You might have yours on the bathroom mirror, beside your computer monitor, on a special board (cork or whatever) or even in the kitchen.

So far, I've been talking about just one card. But the truth of the matter is, you can have as many goal cards as you like and need. Your goals don't all happen at the same time. They don't all manifest right away. So, using goal cards to help you focus on the next goal and the other goals that are going to help you Accomplish Magnificent Things, just makes sense. Make as many as you want to make, I currently have 22.

I'm going to share with you some of the goal cards that I made just last year. Some of these goals have already come into being, others have not as of yet.

In January, I wrote "I am attracting the perfect assistant. She is smart, energetic, loves to work with me and is afford-able. She is so on top of it, I love paying for her. She handles with incredible ease all of my back end projects, as well as has her own wonderful client-loving ideas. She is my right hand, and I feel blessed every day I found her, and so it is." I recently realized that my assistant, Maxine, is that perfect assistant, and I am so thankful that I manifested her.

When I was writing a goal card for this book, I wrote "My book is magnificent, beautiful and successful. It is better than I can even imagine. People can't wait to buy it. It is completely and easily done within a year. People are drawn to it. I can't wait to share it and it provides me so many opportunities."

One about my weight (wow, I am getting really vulnerable sharing my actual goal cards and size here, but it is all in service to you!) reads, "I am a perfect size 10, healthy and happy. I feel sexy, confident and great in and out of my clothes."

When I was seeking new ideal clients I wrote, "My energy and light attracts my ideal clients." When I realized I was putting too much effort into it, and not allowing enough, I wrote, "I am open to receiving the gifts from God and the Universe. My life is easy, calm, exciting, happy, fulfilled, and abundant."

What are you noticing about my goals? They are positive, in the here and the now and done easily. Some may be long, but some can be only a few words.

A few years ago I realized I had a belief that life needed to be hard so that I felt like I really earned things (although I have always worked extremely hard), and that belief put obstacles in my way. I decided I didn't need or want that limited belief in my life anymore so I wrote a goal card that simply said, "My life is easy." Since that day my life has honestly become easier. I read it every day and believe it can be—so it is.

Now it is time for you to write some of your own goal cards. Use the space below to practice a few. Start with a few: one for your life, one for your relationships and one for your career. Then get some cards, my goal cards or whatever you choose to start using as part of your daily routine.

Life:

_____

_____

_____

_____

_____

_____

_____

Relationship:

_____

_____

_____

_____

_____

_____

_____

Career:

_____

_____

_____

_____

_____

_____

The important thing about goal cards is that you need to have faith that these goals will come to pass. Some might say you need to suspend disbelief—but I firmly believe that you need to simply *believe*. Without a firm belief in your goal and that it will be, you'll end up looking backward instead of looking forward. Through belief and intention, you let the Universe fulfill your goal with grace and beauty in each and every moment. It's the feeling and knowledge that whatever I truly desire is already on its way to me, and so it is.

At first you might feel that this is ridiculous and woo-woo. However, simply let go of those notions that hold you back from belief. In fact, I have had some coaches say, "Fake it 'til you make it." As in, pretend to believe until you can and do believe. Soon, when these goals start to come true you will be able to simply trust that it is true, to "Let go and let God."

Chapter 18

Vision Boards

*"Go confidently in the direction of your dreams.
Live the life you have imagined."*
—Henry David Thoreau

One of my all-time favorite exercises is to use a vision board!

All Types will benefit from this exercise, and will likely go about it differently, so let me explain this before we go on.

Intuitive Types love this because it is visual and creative. This will likely be one of your favorite exercises. If you have done it before, great, but do a new one now. In fact, update it constantly. The visual component of this exercise is something you should be updating at least every six months. I will talk more about this in a bit.

Sensing Types love the tactile creativity of the exercise. You will enjoy cutting out the pictures, figuring out where to put them, and how to arrange them. Where you Sensing Types may prefer the specifics and details of the goal cards, this is also an incredibly important exercise to push your big picture thinking.

NPs, as always, will have difficulty finishing the project (but still need to; find a friend to do it with and make a pact you will finish it together).

NJs will need to try not to micromanage the project, and allow for their creativity to be alive.

SJs will need to allow for the creativity of the project to flow, and stop the thinking that it is silly. It will open up a new part of your mind, literally.

SPs will want to just play with the pictures and may not want to finish it. Just finish it already!

I like to think of vision boards as being the goal card's older sibling. The goal card is great for tightly focused goals. However, vision boards allow you to play with pictures and words that create a certain feeling. The vision board is, in essence, a visual of the things you want in your life.

Just like your goal card, the vision board is a daily visual reminder of where you are going and how you want to feel. You can use whatever medium you want to make this vision board. Some people cut up old magazines others find pictures on Pinterest or Google Images and then print them out.

You might think that you need to make a vision board intentionally, looking for specific pictures or images. You can, however, simply allow yourself to feel drawn to images and words and put them together on your vision board.

As a rule, I recommend making a vision board at least once a year, but twice a year is better. I know some people who make a new vision board every quarter or at least update it quarterly. The great thing about vision boards is that the things will start to come true and you can replace them with new, bigger visions.

What you'll need to make your vision board:
- Something to place your images on: corkboard, cardboard, back of a door or my preference, around your full length mirror

- Scissors

- Glue or tape

- Magazines

- Images from Pinterest/Google Images

Here is a picture of one of my recent vision boards. As you can see, I put mine around my full length mirror because I like to see it reflected back at me.

The theme for my vision board had to do with powerful, luminous women. I didn't realize it when I chose the pictures; I simply allowed myself to choose pictures that resonated or spoke to me at the time and just cut them out. Once I was going through them I realized I had a theme—I imagine you will have a similar experience. I then noticed I started feeling lighter and freer and happier. Shortly afterwards, I started to lose the weight that I've been struggling to get rid of. I feel lighter and I know that a part of it is because I see these images in my vision board every single day. It's just like Wallace Wattles says, "the impressing of these images on the mind every day makes an impact on the mind."

Chapter 19

Books

· ·

"The more that you read,
The more things you will know.
The more that you learn,
The more places you'll go."

—*Dr. Suess*

· ·

Books and reading are great ways to explore new ideas and to shift your mindset. That being said, not everyone enjoys sitting down and reading a book. For some, it's too boring to read. For others, they aren't getting enough pretty pictures. Others find it hard to focus on the page, and would far prefer to just listen to a lecture or an audio book. Everyone learns differently, and all those ways are perfectly okay.

That being said, I fully believe that the books that I recommend in my Resources section at the back of this book are great tools to help you shift your mindset. Look through the list, and when you find one that you want to learn more about, find it in the medium that works best for you and your Type.

Chapter 20

Meditation

*"Successful people do
what other people are not willing to do."*
—Unknown

When people hear the word meditation, many images come to mind. Often, there is the image of the Master, seated in a lotus pose with the incense swirling on the breeze in a still, quiet garden. They imagine having to sit still for a long time, being quiet, emptying their mind and chanting mantras in a foreign language. Unfortunately, many Western people (Americans and Europeans) still think of meditation in this way. In fact, I used to hate the word "meditation." The idea of sitting and meditating held absolutely no appeal to me as a strong Extrovert. However, I have learned that there are as many ways to meditate as there are Types of people. Meditation is not one thing for everybody. Meditation for one person might be taking a walk, for another it might be going through a garden, for another it might be sitting outside. You don't have to close your eyes to meditate; you can meditate with your eyes open. You can do guided meditations or un-guided meditations. But, when it comes down to it, meditation is taking the time to be alone, to not talk to others, and get quiet, center yourself and breathe. It is a reflective (looking inward) exercise that can bring a lot of clarity to problems or simply to bring insight.

We all need down time! We can choose to numb out and binge watch Netflix (which has its time and place) but better yet, we can choose to be mindful of our down time and simply meditate. The definition of mindfulness is to pay attention on purpose, so pay attention to your down time and truly enjoy it.

Meditation is a practice of bringing your attention back to your breath, which is the center of all life. We are all bombarded with outside stimuli these days and can lose our primary focus, which should always be us.

It still amazes me how many people find this practice of selecting time that is just for you as being selfish. I truly believe it is selfish not to honor yourself with personal time. We simply cannot be our best selves if we are not grounded in who we are. This entire book is about exactly that, and the practice of meditation is the best of all these techniques. Think of it as time to get reconnected to your core, your breath, you. I like to think of it as grounding your feet in cement. The craziness of our lives, the outside influence and demands upon us can push against us; if we don't have a practice of grounding ourselves to who we are, we can easily get knocked over. But, if our feet are firmly cemented in who we are, things can push us, but we do not fall over. A daily practice of journaling, meditation, visualization, and reading goal cards can help cement your feet. It is another way of thinking of boundaries: we cannot set boundaries for ourselves if we don't know who we are!

Forms of meditation:

Meditation is like a muscle; the more you work out, the stronger you will become. When you are just getting started, your mind will wander often. Don't judge it, just notice it and bring yourself back to the meditation. You will get better, I promise. When I first started meditating, I kind of hated it because I spent so much time judging myself for doing it wrong. Then I realized, as I do with most things, "I am doing it, this is all part of the process. It will never be perfect." The Dalai Lama has even said he still has a wandering mind when meditating. Don't judge yourself; just do it.

Most Extroverts prefer guided visual meditations, especially to start. There are literally thousands on iTunes, but I have provided a few of my favorites at the back of this book. I still use these and love them.

You can meditate anywhere you like. I like to meditate in my imaginary treehouse. You might prefer to meditate in a park; it could be in your own house or it could be by the beach. The important thing is simply for you to feel safe and comfortable so you can enter into that meditative state.

The next thing to consider is time, and choosing the best time for you to meditate. If you're a morning person, waking up a bit earlier to take that time to meditate could help you start the day off well. If you're a night owl, maybe meditating when everyone else is quiet will give you the opportunity to go deep into yourself to get new perspectives and insight. It's tough to meditate when the kids are pulling on you and demanding attention or when your boss is yelling for you to hand over that report or when your partner needs your help with something. Choose your best time and commit to taking that time every day, no matter what, even if it is just a few minutes. I like to spend my few minutes in between clients closing my eyes or looking at the water outside my office and getting myself centered back to my breath. It is the best way to get myself centered so that I can then give my best to my next client. Think about how you could incorporate that into your life with your children, spouse, and clients.

Different meditations lend themselves to different ways and times to do them. One of my friends uses super-short hypnosis meditations (seven minutes long) twice a day—morning and night—to help her get stay focused and to help her feel more positive about her circumstances. Another person I know says that she's joined the "5 a.m." club. This mother and entrepreneur wakes every day at 5 a.m so that she can meditate, exercise and focus on her goals.

No matter what style of meditation you choose, simply taking the time to do this every day can help you take leaps and bounds in the right direction for your life.

Chapter 21

Gratitude Journal

"The day she let go of things that were
weighing her down was the day she began
to shine the brightest."

—*Katrina Mayer*

I have a number of journals going at one time—one for my free writing, another for "aha" business ideas and the last is for my daily gratitude. I start each and every morning doing all three on my big comfy chair with my favorite table next to it, filled with my books, journals, fresh flowers and a lit candle.

A daily gratitude journal can dramatically change your attitude toward your life, yourself, and others. Choosing to see the positive each and every day is a conscious decision, and one I choose to make daily. I suggest you do the same.

When I first started doing this practice I assumed each day would be filled with all the same things: my family, my health, blah, blah, blah. But much to my surprise, I had unique things on my list every single day. There is so much to be grateful for when we take the time to notice it, write it down and spend time paying attention to it. We can also do this practice with our partner. If you find yourself nitpicking every single thing your partner does wrong, start a gratitude journal for all the things they do right, the things you love about them, and it will start to grow. Also, start making a conscious effort to do nice things for them—it could change your relationship!

I simply write a new page each day with the date and "today I am grateful for." Sometimes the list is longer than others, but there is always something on the list.

As I've already talked about before, what we think about all day expands. So if I am thankful that I have enough money to pay a bill that day, even if I don't want to pay it, showing gratitude for having the money will allow it to grow. Remember that positivity begets positivity! Negativity begets negativity. Choose positivity every day!

Chapter 22

Core Desired Feelings

"Being vulnerbale puts me back into a place
of feeling powerful."

—Jessica Butts

This is one of my all-time favorite exercises and practices I have incorporated in my life—it has become a staple. It comes from Danielle LaPorte's book *The Fire Starter Sessions*, and it has to do with core desired feelings (CDFs). If you're a Feeling Type, this is probably one of the best tools to get yourself centered and grounded into who you are. As you do this exercise, you will notice how well they correlate to your Type.

Rather than focusing on a goal, such as one with a date or specific numbers, core desired feelings have to do with how we want to feel in our lives and focusing our intent on how we want to feel. I have found that focusing on my core desired feelings is useful, especially when opportunities or people come into my life which don't resonate with my CDFs. It helps me feel okay with saying "no" to things that I really don't want.

So what is a core desire feeling? It is a feeling that you want to feel in your life. It can be anything, just like you. Your Type will, of course, influence some of those feelings you want to have. So will your personal history. But I encourage you to explore what feelings make you feel good. Take the time to brainstorm.

I want you to do this exercise. Write, while in your Front Seat, all the words/ways you want to feel. Don't judge it—just write and write. Write them all down. If you use the same word twice, or 15 times, I don't care. That is actually part of the exercise. Once you have an exhaustive list, or maybe you only have ten things, go back and see if there are words that came up more than once. Circle the ones that you wrote down multiple times or that you have particular energy around.

If you're not sure what you want to feel, take a look at this list and see which feelings resonate for you:

- Freedom
- Loved
- Inspired/Inspiring
- Happy
- Grateful
- Creative
- Purposeful
- Authentic
- Calm

- Peaceful
- Energetic
- Safe
- Loyal
- Independent
- Safety
- Compassion
- Integrity

You can focus on just a few feelings, or you could have hundreds of them. There is no wrong answer, just the right feeling for you. Write down some of the feelings that repeat in the space following:

_____

_____

_____

_____

_____

_____

_____

Once you've identified a bunch of those feelings, see if you can put them into related categories. You will likely find that some of your feelings are part of a group of related feelings (inspired, creative, open or loving). Let me give you an example of how those core desired feelings look for me:

My biggest core desired feeling is freedom. It is one of the reasons I work for myself. It is one of the reasons I left my job in corporate America. I didn't know this when I was working in that field. But now, it makes sense to me why I can't work a nine to five job; it's because I want to feel free, and I am an Intuitive Type. One of my other core desired feelings is I want to be inspired, and I want to be inspiring. It is something that drives me every single day in my life. When an opportunity comes in and I don't feel inspired or I don't feel the opportunity to be inspiring, I tend to lose interest fairly quickly. I want to have love in my life. I want to feel authentic every single day and I want to feel powerful.

Just like everything else in this book, your core desired feelings will be directly related to your Type, and will be another tool on your roadmap to Living Your Life from the Front Seat.

To help you build out your core desired feelings, here are some examples of the amazing women in my Intuitive group coaching program (personality Types and their core desired feelings):

INTJ – wisdom, respect, love, security, trustworthiness, justice, freedom

INFJ – beauty, health, love, wisdom, justice, integrity

ENTP – health, love, humor, wisdom, integrity

ENFP – freedom, independence, creativity, purposeful work, compassion

ENFJ – freedom, authenticity, love, inspire, powerful

Now that you have identified your own core desired feelings, these will be the gateway to everything that is introduced into your life. New friends, new job, new relationship —everything gets filtered through these feelings because it is how you want to feel. This is taking charge of your life, and what you allow into it based on how you are designing your future and how you want to feel—you are in charge! When I did this exercise, it changed the way I saw almost everything and the new things I was allowing into my life.

I always ask myself when a business opportunity arises or a new person enters into my life:

- Does it allow me to feel free and have the freedom I need and desire?

- Can I be completely authentic with it or the person?

- Do I feel loved and can I freely give love?

- Do I feel inspired and do I get an opportunity to be inspiring?

- Can this person or opportunity allow me to be as powerful as I need to be?

If the answer is "no" to any of these questions then I move on (and you should too based on the items on your own list). If you don't, you will likely regret it later. So, you might as well use this tool because it works! I suggest you make your own questions for your core desired feelings and use them in your life daily. Does your job allow you to have your core desired feelings? Does your spouse make you feel these things? Do you have friends in your life that don't make you feel your core desired feelings? It is time to take inventory and maybe make some changes in your life. I will get to that more in the next section when we start talking about *"How are you going to get there?"* because sometimes you have to make changes in your current situation to get the life you desire. I promise you it will be worth it.

Your feelings are yours. They are okay, and you are okay. I would never judge them, please don't judge yourself for these feelings. They, like your Type, just are. Just like your goals, you can re-explore your core desired feelings as much as you want. You may find, once you get going, that some of your feelings have been validated and met, so now you feel better able to express and ask for the other feelings you know you want in your life. This is all good, and a part of your journey. Enjoy it!

Chapter 23

Like-minded People

"You are the average of the five people
you spend the most time with."
—Jim Rohn

I cannot stress enough how important it is to surround your-self with like-minded people. It's really hard to overcome your past, or to move forward into your goal and future, when you are surrounded with the same people who caused or contributed to your problems now. You need to surround yourself with like-minded people so that you have the support you need to be who you are.

Alcoholics who are in a relationship that contributes to their alcoholism are going to have a much tougher time with getting sober if they stay with their drinking buddies. You may need to see yourself like a recovering alcoholic if you are also in a toxic relationship, or surrounded by people who are contributing to your problem.

One of my clients grew up in a home where she was loved, but she was not allowed to be who she was. Eventually, she married a man who didn't allowed her to be who she was, and then moved to a community where she wasn't allowed to be who she was. She felt like a fake, unappreciated, alone and invisible. By incorporating like-minded people into her life, she is realizing how powerful having a community that understands her, supports her and loves her can be.

Being surrounded with people who believe the same things I believe—who read books that resonate with me—make me feel amazing. I no longer feel alone. I have a community of people that I can be my true self with, without apology. You can also be surrounded with people who think like you do. You don't have to be alone. This community of like-minded people can take many forms.

For some, this is a religious community, where they feel validated and accepted for their beliefs and way of living. For others, it's a social community—where people of similar values and goals can come together to work toward a particular goal. There are Facebook groups for people who have similar values and interests, whether they're radical environmentalists or financial whizzes. There are book clubs, fitness classes, and historical re-enactment groups—whatever excites you and makes you feel more alive, appreciated, connected, and whole. Finding your group of like-minded people can help you express your inner self and be totally authentic.

For the rare Types out there, this will be especially important because we are only 25% of the population. So, we have likely grown up feeling misunderstood or not "gotten" by many people in our lives. Those three Type groups again are:

- Intuitive (N) Types
- Male Feeling (F) Types
- Female Thinking (T) Types

I have started a special group coaching program just for

Intuitive Types because I know how misunderstood I felt for so many years, and how important it was to find like-minded people who really get me. I want the same for other Intuitive Types. If you want more information, you can visit my website (www.jessicabutts.com).

If you're stuck with a group of people who just don't get you, who always make you be something you're not (or that you don't want to be), it's tough to feel validated. You might (and probably will in time) end up losing some of these people who have been a part of your life. That's okay. Sometimes it is time to let go of them and those relationships. It is much easier to do this, however, when you are surrounded by others who think and feel like you do.

If, right now, you don't know of a group of people who have similar beliefs/experiences/goals/values as you, then maybe the problem isn't that there isn't a community for you. Perhaps it is the Universe asking you to be the one to create that group, to be the magnet for others to feel safe to come out and be themselves with you. Yes, it can be frightening to stop hiding (because that's what we do when we're scared). But once you start, more and more people will be drawn to you and your work—and you won't be doing it alone anymore. Be the change you are seeking!

In this section, we have been talking about mindset, taking what we learned about Type and how to Live Your Life from the Front Seat and **doing something with it**. It is possible to shift your mindset. Through this section, we've explored a number of different techniques you can use to accelerate your mind shift and change your life. I have helped my clients use these tools many times, and every time that they diligently use these tools and techniques, I have witnessed astounding, positive impacts in their lives.

All of this is possible if you are in your Front Seat! Remember, our Front Seat is authenticity—our best selves. This is where we can **believe** all this can be! We must know our Types first, so we can start visualizing and designing our life around our Front Seat, the way God made us. If you have done some of these techniques before and they did not work for you, it may be because you were not doing it from your Front Seat. Our Back Seat is fear and doubt; it is yucky, wonky energy. We cannot create the life we want for ourselves if we are constantly in the Back Seat.

Remember to be patient with yourself, and to give yourself (and the Universe) time to bring those changes into reality. It's all about the journey, not necessarily the destination. Use your goal cards and vision board to help you begin your day with intention. Take time to meditate to better understand yourself and get greater clarity. Surround yourself with people who really understand you and who will support you when you need supporting.

In the next chapter, we will to explore how you're going to get to your optimal destination. Then we'll bring all this back together so that you can create an actionable plan to help you Accomplish Magnificent Things by Living Your Life from the Front Seat.

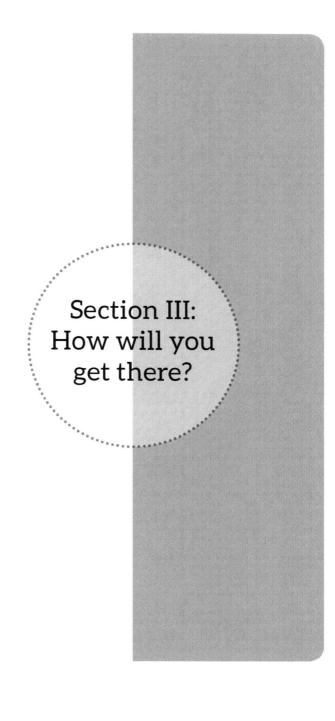

Section III:
How will you
get there?

Chapter 24

Taking Action!

....

"Decide what it is you want.
Write that shit down.
Make a fucking plan.
And...
Work on it.
Every.
Single.
Day."

—*Unknown*

....

We are coming to an end, but nothing in life is complete without taking action!

In the first section, you explored the question *"Who are you?"* You've asked and answered the question of who you are through coming to understand your Innate personality Type, your natural gifts and talents, your Front Seat Drivers and your dreaded Back Seat Drivers. You've discovered who you are through coming to understand your nature and what nurtured you into the person you are today. This is your history, part of what makes you unique, and how you relate to others. All of this is what helps you Live Your Life from the Front Seat. Knowing your Type will also help you understand your strengths and weaknesses around taking action.

In the second section, you started to look forward and ask *"Where are you going?"* By knowing your unique abilities and personality Type, you can stop looking backward in the rearview mirror and turn in the direction of where you want to go. You can decide to change what you are doing now so that you can move forward and Accomplish Magnificent Things. I gave you eight life changing and mindset altering tools to help you design the life you want.

In this last section, we will answer the question of *"How are you going to get there?"* Now that you have new direction in your life, how will you get to your dream life? How will you overcome old patterns, get past road blocks and lift yourself out of a pit? How will you get where you want to go, rather than staying where you are now? The answer is to take action!

> *"You have to act yourself into a new way of being"*
> —*Unknown*

I cannot tell you how many people stay stuck because they don't know who they are and they don't design, visualize and plan a life for themselves. They live a life that others have decided they should live, which I think you would agree is totally crazy. #banishshould

I have mentioned many times throughout this book that this is indeed my story, as I know it is for so many of you as well. I was told to shush, just go along, get your head out of the clouds, get a "real" job, people won't pay for that and are you sure this is what you want to do. I am sure you can think of a few things people have said to you along the way as well.

Why don't you take a moment to write a few of the old beliefs down that we are going to let go, burn, toss out and move past.

_____

_____

_____

Again, these messages come along for the ride in the trunk of our car. As I often say, "our mess is our message" meaning all this crap that happened to you might just be how you can make a difference in this world. Knowing your Innate awesomeness and some of these traumas might just be the key to your brilliance in this world. In fact, I would bet on it, my friends!

Let's return to my equation:

Thoughts + Beliefs + Actions = Your LIFE

It's great for you to explore your thoughts and beliefs, but until you put your plan into action—until there is momentum behind your thinking—nothing is going to happen. You are just being entitled until you take action! The only way for you to get un-stuck and to start to Accomplish Magnificent Things is for you to start doing.

> *"I love to see a young girl go out and grab the world by the lapels. Life's a bitch. You've got to go out and kick ass. "*
> —*Maya Angelou*

Just sitting around and hoping your goal cards will come true and not doing anything about your life is not redesigning your life. You cannot move forward by sitting around, expecting things to come to you. You have to take action. Even the smallest action, done consistently, yields results.

What you do is up to you. When you begin to design a new life for yourself, you might feel stuck, like you're in a rut. If you're not changing anything, you're not going to get new results. You have to change something in order to get a new result.

I am all about action. You cannot and will not get anywhere different in life if you don't take action. We spent the entire last chapter envisioning and designing a new life for you, but sitting around thinking about it isn't enough; you have to take action on those new thoughts.

If you don't **do** the stuff in the previous chapters, all the time you spent reading this book will be a total waste! Even if it is tiny little steps, you must take a step—even just one. Some of you will do this work faster than others; for some of you, this will take months or years, but it is a journey. One that will never end. You must <u>take action</u>.

> *"One Day, you will wake up and there won't be anymore time to do the things you've always wanted. Do it now."*
> —*Paulo Coelho*

One of the things that may be holding you back from moving forward is your relationships. And by relationships, I don't just mean your intimate relationship with your partner, but also with family and friends, as well as your relationship with yourself.

Depending on the kinds of relationships that you have, and how much you're contributing to that mess you currently call your life, you may have many or just a few challenges for you to overcome in order to start moving forward to your dream life.

Back at the end of Section 1, we discussed codependency. Since this chapter is all about taking action, this is a good place to remind you about the power of codependency. Here is a quick reminder of what the tennis court interaction looks like:

Codependent people allow others to control them out of doing what they need to do for themselves, or they are too busy managing and controlling other people to look at their own shit. Both stay stuck.

This chapter is truly about personal responsibility; you will never get anywhere in life if you don't take personal responsibility for your own actions. You choose what you put in your mouth every day. You choose to get up early to do your journaling and mediation. You choose to be nice to the person at the grocery store. You choose to stay in an unhealthy relationship and do nothing about it. You choose to stay in that shitty job and not change your attitude, go back to school or find another one. YOU are in charge of your life (along with God/Universe's help), so you have nobody to blame but yourself if it is not where you want it. Put your big girl panties on and start taking some action towards the life you want to live; please, I implore you. This is for you! I don't even know you, but I want this for you. I want it for everyone.

First and foremost, you must accept responsibility for your own actions that are causing you to feel unhappy and unsatisfied with life. You are not entirely without blame for the mess that your life might be right now. It didn't all happen to you, you helped in some way to create the life that you are living now. You are, in part, responsible for the life you are leading.

Take the time to do the heavy lifting and take responsibility for your thoughts, beliefs and actions that have brought you to where you are today. This isn't an easy thing to do, and it is easy to get caught up in feeling that you're worthless, useless, and stupid.

Stop beating yourself up. Start being kind and loving and saying nice things to yourself.

You can do this, but most of us need help; it is OK to ask for help! I got help; I still get help. You don't have to do this alone; it is much easier and actually more fun to do with someone loving by your side.

Chapter 25

What to do

··

"The only person you are destined to be,
is the person you decide to be"
—*Ralph Waldo Emerson*

··

Now that you've started on this path, it's important to keep going. Most importantly, remember to stay in your Front Seat. Don't let fear and worry throw you into the Back Seat of your car, and playing small.

Having made it this far, you already know that each Type will have ways that they best get into their Front Seat. Each Type will want to do things in a different way, which allows them to Live Life from the Front Seat.

You have the power to create your own life, to choose what you want to do. Remember to keep your Type in mind, so that you can create the life you truly want.

Judging personalities are action takers; they move, they like decisive decisions. You have likely already done some of the suggested activities in Chapter 2. But Js, be open to possibilities. You have a tendency to want it your way, and can often times miss the signs right before you.

Perceiving personalities are slower; they get distracted easily, they like to start projects and then they get bored.

Perceiver, hear me now: get a coach, a good one! Surround yourself with like-minded Judgers that are going to hold you accountable. Pay someone good money to help you, coach you. Get a board of directors or mastermind group that is not going to let you get away with jumping all over the place or not holding you accountable to get stuff done.

Whatever you choose to do, doing it according to your own personality Type will help you. Your action can exist in your business, your family, your health, your fitness, your marriage, your job, anything at all. Just start taking action by doing affirmations, journaling, reading great books, vision boards, goal cards, getting a great therapist or coach, eating great healthy foods, moving your body and taking care of your vessel that houses your awesome soul. Here are some specific tips:

- Keep reading books that help you deal with your specific challenges

- Write daily in your gratitude journal

- Create a vision board and keep it updated

- Constantly filter things through your core desired feelings

- Read about your personality Type often to remind yourself of how awesome you are

- Keep on updated list of Front Seat Activities and do them

- Keep a journal to help you work through your issues

- Spend time with amazing friends who support you in your new paradigm

- Write and read your goal cards daily

- Take time to visualize and meditate

- Don't do stuff you suck at anymore (Drunk Uncle and Baby in the Back Seat stuff)

- Work through your traumas with a super therapist or coach

This may seem like a lot, but I promise you, once you start doing these things, they will simply become a normal and necessary part of your day; one you will love and look forward to. Until you do this, and continue on this path, you're just going to end up going back to the same patterns that you've been stuck in all these years.

Remember also that taking action may be things that you stop doing, such as things that don't align with your core desired feelings, or anything in your Back Seat! They can also be actions that you begin in order to replace actions which have kept you out of your Front Seat. If it makes you truly happy, do it.

Writing this book was not easy. It was hard work writing a book, but I don't want another person wasting their life doing things they are not meant to be doing like I did for so many years. Living an incongruent life is painful. I know, I did it for 20 years. It almost broke me. I want something different for you. That is why I wrote this book; it is why I do the work I do. You can do this!!! I did it, and so can you. I promise.

You get one life my friends, this is it. Live it full out. That starts by taking small steps every single day that get you moving in the right direction. While you will still occasionally have moments when you think you're back in your old life, those moments will become fewer and fewer as you progress. As you start to take steps in the direction of Living Your Life from the Front Seat, the Universe will reward you. Watch for it, notice it (remember your gratitude journal), it will happen.

You are now ready to go forward to Live Your Life from the Front Seat! I have every confidence in you that, once you get in the Driver's seat, and begin to put your beliefs into action, you will end up at the destination you've decided upon and Accomplish Magnificent Things.

Now, you're ready to hit the road and enjoy your journey as you travel through life in your Front Seat!

"Go confidently in the direction of your dreams. Live the life you have imagined."
—Henry David Thoreau

About the author

Jessica is a sassy psychotherapist and life fulfillment Coach and Myers-Briggs expert who believes in "telling it like it is" while inspiring everyone to Accomplish Magnificent Things by embracing their innateness. She has a private practice just outside of Seattle, WA, and travels the country teaching her Live Your Life from the Front Seat method. She is passionate about personal development, her work, traveling, deep connections with those in her life, being a vegetarian, self expression in any form possible, and of course her beloved Boston Terrier, Tucker.

Jessica believes in giving back. She is donating a portion of the proceeds from this book to a local (Seattle) organization that fights tirelessly for those with no voice, the animals. Thank you, Erica Farnsworth, for the work you do for them.

Action for Animals
www.actionforanimals.com

Resources

Codependent No More - Melody Beattie

The Language of Letting Go - Melody Beattie

The Fire Starter Sessions - Danielle LaPorte

The Big Leap - Gay Hendricks

The Four Agreements - Don Miguel Ruiz

Please Understand Me - David Keirsey

Goal Cards - www.jessicabutts.com

Whole Letter Type - www.jessicabutts.com

Ask and it is Given - Abraham Hicks

Man's Search for Meaning - Viktor Frankl

Life Visualization iTunes Meditation - Lisa Guyman

26198331R00137

Made in the USA
San Bernardino, CA
21 November 2015